PRAIS

HELLO A

MY OLD FRIEND

"This is not a book about cancer, but it is. This is not a book about relationships, but it is. It is a book about anxiety, but it is more than that: through Natalie's experiences and insights, we understand better how this concept of anxiety creeps into all aspects of our lives—when facing a medical challenge, in our marriages, friendships, and all the spaces in between. Everyone knows something about anxiety—yet so many still struggle and are baffled by it—why is this? Natalie, who I am lucky to call a professional peer and dear friend, covers the concept of anxiety in a totally accessible way and provides insights from both personal and professional perspectives. It is what I would call elegantly simple—which is a true compliment in this day of flashy results and overzealous promises to find a quick fix.

"Bravo, Natalie, for cutting through it all and sharing your wisdom!

"Don't miss this book!"

—Patricia Mowry-Cavanaugh, LPC, PhD
Senior Vice President of Clinical Services
at Health Connect America

"Natalie Kohlhaas, a seasoned therapist whose own prior trauma, fear, and feelings of anxiety informs her expertise and care for clients. She provides a book that could not come at a more traumatic, fearful, and anxiety-ridden time in most of our lives and at a time that her expertise is needed more by the most of us. I am certain that the stories that Natalie tells will resonate with you, and her wisdom will set you on a course to health and well-being."

—Eve Heemann Byrd, MPH, DNP, FNP-BC, PMH CNS
Director, The Carter Center Mental Health Program

"Anxiety is the condition of the modern age, and Natalie Kohlhaas is the master clinical therapist who can best help all of us in understanding it, managing it, and even appreciating some of its paradoxical virtues. She writes with humor, wisdom, and empathy that comes from her own episodes of personal trauma. Anxious humans—which is to say all of us—will benefit immensely from the insight and advice that Natalie Kohlhaas offers."

—Geoffrey Kabaservice, BA, MPhil, PhD
New York Times **Author**
Director of political studies at the
Niskanen Center in Washington, DC

Hello Anxiety, My Old Friend

Hello Anxiety, My Old Friend

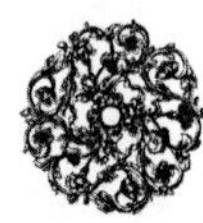

Harness Your Invisible Superpower

Sit on the Couch
with Anxiety Specialist

Natalie Kohlhaas

Master Clinical Therapist
MA, LPC, NCC, CPCS, C.Ht

BOOKLOGIX®
Alpharetta, GA

Some names and identifying details have been changed to protect the privacy of individuals. The author has tried to recreate events, locations, and conversations from her memories of them. In some instances, in order to maintain their anonymity, the author has changed the names of individuals and places. The resources contained within this book are provided for informational purposes only and should not be used to replace the specialized training and professional judgment of a healthcare or mental healthcare professional. Author and the publisher of this work cannot be held responsible for the use of the information provided. Always consult a licensed mental health professional before making any decision regarding treatment of yourself or others.

ISBN: 978-1-6653-0539-6 - Paperback
ISBN: 978-1-6653-0540-2 - Hardcover
eISBN: 978-1-6653-0541-9 - ePub

♾This paper meets the requirements of ANSI/NISO Z39.48-1992 (Permanence of Paper)

Cover picture by Sandra Meyer, www.sandrameyergallery.com

Author photo by Leticia Andrade, www.lehphoto.com

0 1 1 9 2 3

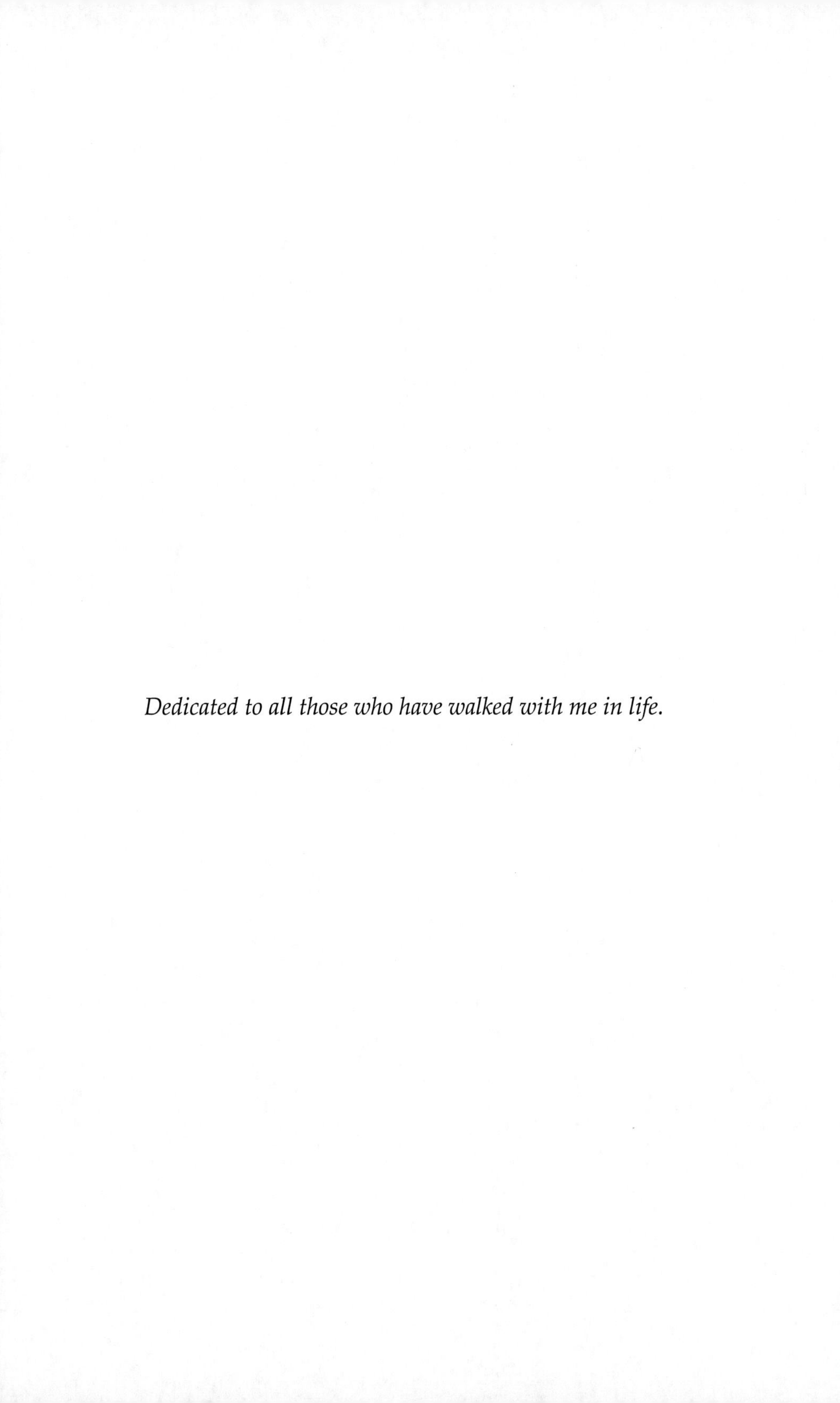

Dedicated to all those who have walked with me in life.

Owning your own story is the bravest thing you'll ever do.
—Brené Brown

CONTENTS

Prologue

AWAKENING

May you sleep with the angels who give you strength to live another day.

—Awesoroo.com

Light slowly and gently seeps in fuzzy around the edges as my eyes begin to focus. His eyes are gentle, but as I take him in, I see concern. Tiredness seeps out from around his edges—rumpled clothing, bags and laptops, fast food nearby. Around me, the room gradually grows and clears as the sunlight streams in from the window. My mind feels available and calm as my husband's presence soothes me.

Suddenly, I'm awake. I'm in the hospital. Confusion begins to build.

Wait. I'm supposed to be at home. Not here. Not in the hospital. My mind reaches for anything in the room that feels familiar.

"What day is it?"

My husband's voice disrupts my search for comfort. "Do you remember what day it is?"

I look around. I see a bulletin board on the wall saying "Thursday."

Well, it must be Thursday. But somehow, it doesn't seem like it is Thursday. Perhaps they have the wrong date listed?

Tentatively, I respond, "Thursday?"

My husband smiles and nods.

Yes. Relief, I gave him the right answer.

But wait . . . this makes no sense. It was Friday. Why is it Thursday? Surgery was on Friday. I close my eyes as I rest into this thought. *Thursday, Thursday . . .*

I open my eyes and see the sign on the wall stating it is Thursday.

"Is today Thursday?" I ask when I once again open my eyes.

Gentle eyes, tired and filled with love, reassure me, "Yes, it is Thursday. You asked me that. Do you remember asking me?"

Hmm, this doesn't make sense to me. It was just Friday. When I had surgery, it was Friday.

I look at my husband. His presence is soothing. He is here with me, solid, stable. I know I don't need to worry. Yes, I don't need to worry. I can relax. I can drift. My mind relaxes and drifts off.

Light gently and slowly seeps in fuzzy around the edges as my eyes try to focus. I open my eyes and see my husband.

"What day is it?"

CHAPTER ONE

A TIGER'S TALE

The spiritual journey is the unlearning of fear and the acceptance of love.

—Marianne Williamson

I have been working with Anxiety for twenty-plus years. And it still amazes me how I can talk to a client who has experienced panic attacks, gone to therapy, and yet does not know why their body is presumably putting them through hell. So one of the first things I do is something known as psychoeducation. Psychoeducation provides me an opportunity to explain why their body is responding in a way that feels deliberately harmful.

To do this, I have them go on a journey with me.

TIME MACHINE

Imagine we are going back in time. Try to think of ourselves as hunters and gatherers living in a beautiful cave that is clean and well maintained—surrounded by woods that slowly change and morph into brush and then an open field. The cave feels cool and inviting in the heat yet warm and comforting in the winter cold. On this day—a beautiful late spring day—it is a day that we have been waiting for, for today, the berries will be fully ripe and ready to pick. We can see them in our mind's eye, sweet, staining our fingers and tantalizing our tongues.

The trees, large and stable about us, enfold around the cave. We head into the woods, making our way to the berry bushes that lie outside the woods and near the open field. The day is glorious. The sky is a soft blue, speckled with puffy white clouds slowly passing overhead, and we know the berries will taste amazing. There will be others who also have come out to gather the sweetness nestled in the bushes. They are from neighboring caves, and though we know them, they are not truly part of our tribe. Enjoying their company, we appreciate them, but we are not tied together. We are more focused on ourselves and our need to gather the warm taste of late-spring sweetness.

Beaming down from overhead, the sun warms us. The smell of the tall grass shifts and moves, swaying gently in the breeze as it crosses to our noses while we collect the warm fruit in leaves.

Suddenly, we hear a strange noise . . .

We do not know from where the sound has come. It definitely was not the sound of the wind or the trees. Now, we are not the type of individuals who think, "Oh, that was nothing. We should just enjoy the beautiful sky and puffy clouds." Instead, we are the type who think, "Oh no, that sounded bad."

But no one else seems to be worried. The others continue to enjoy the weather, the butterflies in the field, and the fresh air swirling around as they pick their berries. You and I look around, taking in the mood among those nearby, and decide that maybe we should also not worry and instead choose to keep gathering the fruit. Yet, once again, moments later, we hear a strange, upsetting, and concerning sound.

Okay. That's it for us. We decide we are out of there.

We are not those happy-go-lucky individuals who sit around saying, "But the sky is blue, and the clouds are puffy, all is right in the world." Instead, we are the type of people who worry and say, "Yes, but what if? What if something is wrong? What if this is something that is going to eat us? What if that headache is a tumor?"

So, we start to gather our stuff and head back toward the cave into the woods. Folding our berries in the large leaves we have brought with us, we look back across the field. Looking over our shoulders, what do we see? A large saber-tooth tiger tail is waving above the grass.

Immediately, our hearts start to beat out of our chests!

Our hearts know this is a threat and instantaneously begin to pump a lot of blood into our bodies so we can RUN! The next thing that goes off is the internal message, "Run, run away." This is the beginning of what people often feel when they experience what they know as panic. The heart rate goes up, they get antsy, feeling like they need to leave. We have to run, run, RUN away!

As we start to run, looking back over the grassy field where the butterflies were dancing over the grass, we see the tiger crouched to attack. We find he has struck the rose-colored-glass neighbors who thought all is right in the world with nothing to worry about. Sadly, for them, they are no longer here to pass on their knowledge and feelings to the next generations. But this is good news for us. It allows us more time to run and get away. This also means that our DNA will hopefully be passed down to other individuals, our children, and our youth if we survive. This also ensures the emotional reaction of feeling worried and concerned when there is any type of threat will also be passed down from generation to generation.

We are running as fast as we can, our hearts are pumping, our legs are moving, and now our lungs are filling with the fresh air as we begin to breathe fast and shallow into our chests, not our bellies. The air moves into our bloodstream, and our brains know instinctively that we need to take small quick breaths. We find we begin to sweat as the smell of our bodies fills the air. Our quick, shallow, fast breath feels strange and constricted in our chests. We need to get oxygen to our muscles, and wisely our bodies know this as they continue to increase the rate of the breaths we take. This type of breathing adds oxygen to the blood so our largest muscles, the legs, get the energy they need while the sweat cools our bodies.

Hyperventilation is a prevalent panic symptom; it occurs when a person breathes out too much carbon dioxide (CO_2). However, your body actually needs CO_2. So, hyperventilation (breathing too fast or taking deeper breaths than you need) can cause several symptoms, one of which is dilating your blood vessels and causing your fingers to tingle. Yet, without all of this extra oxygen, we would not be able to keep up the pace needed to get back to our cave. So, our heart is pumping, our legs are running, and we are breathing with shallow, quick breaths, all the while our bodies are sweating to keep us cool.

The saber-tooth tiger has picked up on the smell of our sweat, and it has seen us fleeing. We are the moving targets that need to be taken down. The tiger zones in on our movement, and we find ourselves going into high activation. Immediately, our brains and bodies go into survival mode. How can I save them both? What if we run and the tiger bites an arm or hand, and we bleed to death? What if we bleed out and die? What if we are never able to tell our children to listen to the noises? What if . . . what if . . . ?

Our body knows it needs to keep us alive, so it begins to move all the blood from our hands and arms into the trunks of our bodies. This does two things: One, it helps to keep all of our organs fed with oxygen-rich blood—the organs we will need to live; the organs we need to breathe, pump our blood, and use to filter our internal environment. But two, it also allows us to remain alive if our extremities are attacked. We will not bleed out if we are bitten on our hands or arm as there will be little blood in these extremities.

The blood has moved to the center of our body, allowing us to get to safety. Our body is going into fight-or-flight mode, and that means adrenaline is coursing through our veins all the time. One of this system's effects is to take blood away from unimportant, life-sustaining areas and move it quickly through the heart. This movement can cause your fingers to be a bit colder and may lead to tingling sensations. This is why those who have panic attacks will often find their arms are going numb, their hands are going cold, and they mistake this protective mechanism for a heart attack.

So, we are pumping a lot of blood, running, sweating, breathing fast, and moving our blood supply into our central chest and core. We are whizzing past the trees, jumping over the debris. But we still need to move faster!

Our body is working hard, trying to decide how to get us to run faster. Instead, it decides to start shutting down parts of the body that are unnecessary in this moment to survive. Those parts use energy, causing us to overwork as we run. We definitely do not need to be digesting our berries. So, the body shuts down our stomachs allowing us to use this energy to run even faster. Once this happens, we notice our stomachs feel like we have a rock inside. This experience is why many people feel butterflies or a heaviness in their stomach when having a panic attack. Now, the stomach can only feel stomach acid as a tangible presence. The Fear response releases a stress hormone (cortisol), which causes the body to produce extra levels of stomach acid. That acidity causes the lining of the esophagus to become irritated, and this can lead to stomach pain, nausea, vomiting, and in severe cases, stress-induced ulcers.

Stress can affect digestion and what nutrients the intestines absorb. Gas production related to nutrient absorption may decrease. While this may not seem helpful, our brain and our body are working hard to protect us. Shutting down the stomach gives us a small amount of energy to run even faster, similar to the energy we receive from manmade cortisol, cortisone. The faster we can go, the more distance we put between us and harm.

But we can only run so fast. Probably not as quickly as the

tiger, so our brains decide there is only one other thing they can do. They need to work on slowing the tiger down. So, it chooses to lessen the weight we are carrying and have the tiger slow down simultaneously.

Our bodies start to empty the extra weight. Bowels are released as poop and pee begin to hit the ground. The stomach propels the berries into the debris as we run for our lives from the tiger. These releases help to lighten the load within our bodies and, more importantly, slow down the tiger. Those who experience intense emotions such as Fear may often feel nauseous. It may come as little surprise that this type of Fear may contribute to the development of irritable bowel syndrome (IBS), also known as "spastic colon."

IBS is a chronic condition that causes bloating, gastrointestinal discomforts, erratic bowel movements, chronic abdominal pain, diarrhea, and constipation. It is a definite unpleasant experience, yet our body knows it is more important to stay alive, so it works to create a diversion.

Just like a dog who will stop and smell where another animal has marked its territory, so does the tiger. It will stop and smell and investigate. Maybe they have dropped a young'un? This is why those who are experiencing Anxiety often have irritable bowel syndrome or experience a desire to use the restroom more frequently when they are worried. The continuation of this stress changes their hormone production, alters their immune system, and in some cases, upsets their digestive tract. And still, the brain knows this mechanism allows for a few extra moments needed to get away. The brain is trying to help.

The sympathetic nervous system has signaled the adrenal glands to release adrenaline hormones (epinephrine) and cortisol. Together, with direct actions of autonomic nerves, these hormones cause the heart to beat faster, respiration rate to increase, blood vessels in the arms and legs to dilate, the digestive process to change, and glucose levels (sugar energy) in the bloodstream to increase to deal with the emergency.

Here we are, heart pounding, breathing fast, sweating, running, moving our blood around, shutting down body organs, and emptying our stomachs and bowels. Our only focus is "GET TO THE CAVE." We do not see the birds, the squirrels, the berries. We experience a narrowing of our senses, a phenomenon known as derealization. Our vision contracts. We are only able to see the route ahead to the cave. Our vision reduces, and we may even experience a ringing in the ears, not taking in any sounds except focusing on our final destination, dizziness, and lightheadedness as blood moves out of the brain into our core. Our brain and body's focus are currently in overload to keep us safe, keep us alive, and protect us. Individuals in survival mode often will experience a loss of visual range, a ringing sensation in the ears, feeling dizzy, and overwhelmed.

Finally, we arrive! We are at the cave! We push our rock in front of the opening, grab our chest, and take a deep, loud, overly big breath! Clutching our chest, we inhale deeply, taking in the air as we hold our breath, gasping and releasing it noisily out through our mouths.

We breathe fully and loudly, taking in deep, powerful belly breaths. They come in, and we gasp, holding our breath as we try to "catch" the air around us. In and out, we breathe deeply, slowly, and noisily.

In and out, in and out the breath comes deeply and noisily.

We are elated to have made it to safety. We are in one piece.

Exhausted and overwhelmed, our body knows all of these protective measures went off so quickly and were very aggressive on our system. Now that we are out of danger, it needs to settle back down slowly. Slowly, so it does not cause more distress. Starting up all of these emergency systems in order to keep us alive was not only tasking but also physically and mentally exhausting. Our deep belly breathing—the type where we are holding it as if to catch our breath and then deploying it noisily, releasing it out into the safety of our cave—signals to our body that WE ARE SAFE.

Our body knows it needs to come back online gradually. The primary reason is so we do not exit the cave too early. If we did, the tiger might still be there; it could be waiting for us, pacing back and forth in the trees. Also, our body used so much energy to get us to safety, and in such a distressful way, it does not want to cause more upheaval as it comes back to a place of rest. More angst would be so difficult for us to handle, which is the opposite of what our body wants. Remember, your body wants what is best. It wants you to be safe, to be able to live yet another day. It will slowly begin to relax and settle down, slowly and evenly, for over twenty minutes.

This is why when I have individuals who are experiencing panic, I have them learn and work on inhaling deep belly breaths. These breaths push the lungs and stomach into the spine, applying pressure onto the vagal nerve, which signals to our brains and bodies it is time to reestablish homeostasis to the overworked systems. What is the vagal nerve? It is the off switch used by the body to signal to the brain "all is okay." It allows us to reestablish calm and reset the autonomic nervous system. This process takes approximately twenty minutes—again, time to keep us safe, slowly allowing the body to reach for a sense of relief.

So, as you can see, your body and brain think they are helping you when you have an attack. They are not working against you. They are working for you. Your body believes it is keeping you safe. Whatever means you use to reestablish your bodies reset will take time. It is not instantaneous for a necessary reason.

I have found individuals who often use their breath to settle their system typically do not take in enough deep breaths, use belly breathing incorrectly, or do not feel their lungs press against their spine. They also often take three breaths and say, "It's not working!" and stop before they can calm their system into a place of relief. I work with clients to breathe in a way that their system can regain balance. But note, this is not a silver bullet. There is more than the breath that needs to be addressed.

Sadly today, people see saber-tooth tigers where there aren't any. In addition, our brain, which is prone to imagine the worst from the DNA passed down from generations and generations of previous worriers, becomes confused. Thus, individuals run from something that does not exist, compounded by traumas that they have experienced. They misread and notice a feeling incorrectly. They fail to discern that there is no tiger. They begin to react to their biological system rather than respond to accurate information. In today's world, we often mistake everything as the imaginary tiger without becoming curious.

Given our past, it makes sense we would be hesitant to become curious. Yet in today's world, pause, thought, curiosity, and action can create amazing outcomes. We are no longer in the world of caves, and tigers eating our neighbors. While we may think or feel this is true, the world has changed and we have the ability to update our understanding.

Explanation of this process allows clients to see that their feelings of panic are the body's way to help, not hurt. In today's world, the imaginary tiger is FEAR. Fear tells us to run from our lives and our experiences. Fear wants us to avoid or react in order to continue the fear. Fear is an expert at creating false evidence that appears real. Thoughts of Fear can create emotional pain which keeps us locked in a past that no longer exists.

Anxiety, though, is different. People often think Fear and Anxiety are the same emotions. They are not the same. Anxiety actually wants us to enjoy our lives and live it to the fullest, not put us through hell. Whereas Fear wants us to run from our lives and sit in a cave with no one, no life, no berries. Yet, because we no longer have saber-tooth tigers, we need to recognize that the tiger has now turned into a thought. It is in our imagination.

Another way to think about this is each time we choose to run and listen to our thought of "what if" without seeing the tiger's tail, we are now heading away from the cave and we are running toward the tiger, toward the scary thoughts and into past programming. We are now running away from our values, from learning and discovering ourselves. But when we run away from our values and ourselves, Anxiety will be present, providing opportunity to correct our course and find our truth.

In today's world, our Anxiety has taken on a new role. Where we once listened to the *feeling* of the tiger, we now can see how Anxiety is trying to get us to address a feeling without information, so we are not misled to run from an imaginary tiger. When we listen to the *feeling* only, without information, we run into danger, not away from danger—the real danger in today's world is losing ourselves, the danger of depression, the danger of emotional pain. We become confused and think we need to control the world around us in order to protect ourselves and keep safe. Our friend Anxiety is here to help harness the world of emotions inside and redirect us toward true internal control.

In this book, we will discuss feelings, what Anxiety is, what it is not, and how Anxiety is your superpower. The superpower we have pushed away, tried to ignore, and overlooked.

For those who run from the imaginary tiger, listen to the incorrect feeling directing you. Notice the loss of control that Fear has imposed. When you listen to Fear, your world will be smaller and the sweetness of life will be removed like the berries you deserve.

Those who mistake Anxiety as the enemy will often encounter the following experiences:

- Joint pain
- Coughing
- Stomach pain and discomfort
- Migraines
- Muscle spasms
- Tension headaches
- Stomach tension
- Buzzing in the ears
- Ringing in the ears

- Fullness in the ears and head
- Night sweats
- Lump in the throat
- Blurred vision
- Hypersensitivity to smells
- Hypersensitivity to one's own body sensations
- Social withdrawal
- Lip biting
- Fear of talking
- Fear of going crazy
- Lethargy/euphoria
- Increased fear and fearful thoughts
- Changes in perception
- Derealization
- Dream overload
- Crying

It is important to note that Fear genuinely alters the way your body works, and long-term stress can alter hormones, tense muscles, and the way the brain fires. All of these issues simply don't repair themselves immediately when the Fear goes away. Fear may cause your hormones, muscles, neurotransmitters, and more to stay out of balance, perpetuating these feelings and issues till you are able to regulate the Fear and find homeostasis.

As we can see, stress is a complex disorder. It affects not only the mind but also the body. It is the stress placed on the body and the chemical changes due to that stress that leads to changes in the body. Physical changes are evident hormonally, chemically, and within the DNA itself when individuals experience continued high-stress levels.

For more information, go to www.HelloAnxiety.net and check out our seven-day personal retreat and experience a moment of calm. For coupon-code information on this course, check out the website.

CHAPTER TWO

CHASED BY THE TIGER

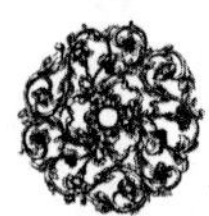

It is not death, but dying, which is terrible.

—Henry Fielding

Forwarded Email Message:

For those who are unaware, a brief recap: On Friday, at 12:40 a.m., Natalie suffered a pulmonary embolism resulting in cardiac arrest. Paramedics were with her when she went into arrest. The medical staff was able to resurrect her at the hospital. She was placed into a medically induced coma and was put into therapeutic hypothermia in the ICU to help her body decrease degeneration. We don't know if she will be with us much longer—

It was a Friday, my eyes were closed, my breath slow and calm. I was centered in a meditation. On the TV was the "CARE" channel where they play calming music and have beautiful pictures of nature flash across the screen.

I don't remember the doctor coming in to get me. I don't remember the ride on the gurney down the hall. I don't even remember them giving me any pain medication or putting me under. I do remember sitting in the waiting area for surgery, legs crossed, gown strewn around my body, the clatter of voices and shoes as staff moved among rooms. I wanted to talk with the doctor before the surgery, to remind her to let me know when I was going to be given anesthesia so I didn't keep talking during the surgery. Apparently, I had sung a song to the surgery team last time I was under.

This time there was no singing at the hospital. I'd apparently suffered a massive pulmonary embolism. The embolism filled both chambers of my heart, closing off my lungs, and shut down my system. The main right and left chamber of the heart filled as the blood clot expanded like cigar smoke filling every crevice and opening. This type of clot is named a "saddle embolism" because it looks like a large saddle on an X-ray.

The embolism caused me to suffer a cardiac arrest. It filled both chambers of my heart and each lobe of my lungs, blocking oxygen from moving into and through my body. My body had to decide. If it was to keep pumping my heart, the embolism would enter my brain. If it entered my brain, I would die. But our bodies love us and are constantly trying to save our silly selves. So, it made a drastic decision: stop the heart from pumping and ultimately shut down my system. My respiration stopped. My heart stopped. All oxygen to the body stopped.

Hypoxia is a condition that occurs when there is not enough oxygen circulating throughout the body to reach all the tissues and organs. This lack of oxygen started to shut down my organs as the decrease worked its way through my body. The longer I was unable to clear the embolism, the faster I was failing. Ischemia, an inadequate supply of oxygen, began to affect my organs. Everything began to break down. Brain connections started to unravel. The brain began to crash. Organs started to fail. The longer I went without oxygen, the more everything withered. I was dying.

How many times had I been here? It seems as though I have been moving against death for years. Even though my body was compromised, my spirit knew this was definitely not "my time." Multiple situations in my life have pressed on me and moved me to understand my sense of control. I have learned how to outrun the tiger. I have learned when the tiger is not real. I have learned to listen to my friend Anxiety and recognize I do have the ability to control the imaginary tiger within. I have passed along to my clients what I have learned, and now I will share it with you in this book.

A dear friend with whom I am deeply connected shared her experience about the night after the embolism. She awoke at 3:00 a.m., "the witching hour" for those of us who understand this wakeful time. She was in a dead sleep when my voice came across her dreams screaming—very loud screaming, loud and deafening. She sat straight up in her bed, her body tense and immediately alert. She could see me far away and small in the distance. But my voice was strong. My voice was clear. My voice was pissed. I was there screaming, "F**k, fu*k!" over and over, louder and louder.

She knew deep within her soul: I was not moving "toward the light." I was pissed, and I was fighting. The tiger was chasing me down, but she was confident I was not giving up. The fight was still on. She could feel I was filled with energy, and that energy would help me find my way back, allowing my struggling body to try and reset.

She knew I was still here—an invisible superpower directing her from within.

Anxiety let her know I was still here, I was fighting. I was.

It was a miracle, but not the first one.

MIRACLE ONE

CHAPTER THREE

THE GIRL WITH NINE LIVES

Loving your body doesn't have to be conditional.

—Christina Costa

Historians say the Egyptians revered the number nine because they associated it with their sun god, Atum-Ra. According to one version, Ra gave birth to eight other gods. Since Ra often took the form of a cat, people began associating nine lives (Ra plus eight) with feline longevity.

Nine is also a magical number—because cats have been both worshipped and feared throughout the ages for being magical, this could partly be why cats are attributed with having nine lives. According to ancient Greeks, the number nine referred to the trinity of all trinities: a mystic number that invokes tradition and religion.

I remember telling people that if I lived during any other time, I most likely would be dead. I would not have survived. If I lived during caveman times, I would have aimlessly wandered along and most likely would have tumbled down a sheer rock face or have been eaten by a bear. My eyesight was so bad that I saw as though looking through an impressionistic painting—a canvas of everyday beautifully smudged watercolors. It is simultaneously stunning and disconcerting, because of this experience, it is commonplace for me to remember the colors people wear and the way their gait moves in order to recognize them when I don't have on my glasses.

If, somehow, I had managed to survive caveman times, I don't believe I would have made it through the birth of our first child. My firstborn was not only in a breech position but was also being held in a pouch. Yes, a pouch. In my womb, there was a formation of skin that looked very much like what we understand a kangaroo pouch to be. This formation kept my first child in place, allowing him to sit straight up in a crossed-legged, Indian-type position. He was held safe and secure but not able to drop, rotate, or be born naturally. Before we knew what was holding our beautiful son, my doctors gave me the option of trying to turn him in my belly before birth. They said they could push, manipulate, and see if they could get his head into the downward position. It sounded horrible.

"That sounds painful. Will it hurt?"

Her response, "Oh, yes, a lot."

It was not until I was in surgery for my first C-section that my strange pouch was discovered. My doctor was amazed; they had never seen anything like it before. In fact, they asked if I would be willing to have the information written up and posted in a medical journal—could they do a study on me?

Well, sure. Why not?

How thankful I am that I live during this time!

My first recognition that life is an expression of energy and relationships was not with my own children's births but my own. My birth took place internationally. I remember hearing my mother tell the story of my birth to a friend when I was young. The story goes that my mother went into labor early. After arriving at the hospital, the doctors deemed that while it was not yet time, she was already dilating. They pulled my father aside and told him to help his wife. To do so, he needed to push the delivery along by taking my mother for a car ride over a very bumpy road (early labor induction). The two of them got back into the car as my dad drove her over railroad tracks and potholes until they arrived back at the house; sure enough, it was time for them to turn right back around and go back to the hospital. My mother's water had broken, everything started to move, and the contractions began to come quickly.

Once at the hospital, it was not smooth sailing. With my father safely sent off to the waiting room, my mother had to experience a complicated birth alone. I, too, was in a breech position. The umbilical cord was wrapped around my neck, strangling me and creating hypoxia in my system. My organs were being starved of blood and oxygen, and if my mother continued to push, I would not survive. Just like with my embolism, a decision needed to be made. Do not push. Do not continue to move things along, or death will result. I was coming out backward. My bottom was where my head should be, the cord was wrapped around my neck, and they told my mother I would strangle myself to death before I entered this world unless she was able to stop her contractions. My mother remembers having to pant and endure the pain for what felt like hours until they were finally able to rotate me inside her belly, reach in, and remove the cord from my neck.

She stopped working with her contractions and allowed me to enter this world. Out I came, held up in the doctor's nimble hands, trembling and crying, small, and alive. I was okay. But I was so little. I was so little my mother told me that she could not find clothes to fit me. She had to go to specialty stores and buy doll clothes to fit my small yet amazingly formed frame. I was this tiny, itty-bitty thing, surrounded by such a huge world, but happy to be here and in it.

I recently asked my father if he remembered the exact time I was born. He didn't remember, except that it was after midnight. He had been sitting with all the other fathers, banished to the waiting room. They were pacing, grumbling with nervous energy that filled the space between each man as it mingled with cigar smoke circling around the room. The smoke expanded as it landed on jackets, ties, and polished shoes. It filled each space as it combined with sweat and anticipation. When my father leaned over and asked the cigar smoker if he was expecting his first child, the man laughed and said, "Oh no, this is my fourth!"

It wasn't until the staff brought me out for my father to see, that he was finally able to breathe. Now he could relax, settling into the birth of his child, and rejoice in his family safe in the cave. A girl, just like he wanted! Counting each finger, he was able to hold me swathed in blankets, surrounded by that newborn smell, clean and fresh in comparison to the room around him. He held me briefly before I was whisked off, and he, too, was sent away to have dinner.

It was a different time. Men were relegated to the waiting rooms, off to the bars, or sent to go get some dinner. The doctors would tell the men, "Go out. We will let you know when it's over."

It had just begun.

CHAPTER FOUR

LISTENING TO YOUR HEART

We suffer more often in imagination than in reality.

—Seneca

The most well-known therapy for helping Anxiety is Cognitive Behavioral Therapy (CBT). CBT allows us to investigate and ask questions that help keep us centered in our truth. CBT helps us uncover belief systems that we have, either consciously or subconsciously, engrained from our past. These beliefs are the things that, for whatever reason, we continue to feed and nurture even when they no longer fit who we are. They dictate our behaviors. Know your superpower Anxiety is present when these beliefs and behaviors need to be corrected.

These old beliefs are the things that plague us and that our internal nemesis, Fear, pushes us to feed. When one of these beliefs is being fed, we feel uncomfortable or worried or concerned or judged or anxious.

I often explain these old beliefs to clients, like clothing that we loved when we were little. It is the outfit that we felt comfortable in, or we would wear over and over again. It is the outfit that we fit into beautifully as a child. It served us so well and kept us as safe as possible. Yet, just like an outfit we wore when we were young, it doesn't fit us now. No matter that it was our favorite or however absolutely familiar it was, it is now too small and no longer fits who we are today.

If we were to wear the outfit we wore when we were, say, six years old, it would look horrid on us now. Our arms would tear through the seams, pressing tightly against the fabric; our legs and chest would be confined. It would be terribly uncomfortable. This is the same uneasy feeling we now get when Anxiety is attempting to get our attention. Anxiety wants us to see when we are using an outdated belief that no longer fits us. A thought that does not express our heart, move us to grow, uplift our spirit, hear a compliment, or reach for the unknown.

As we go through life, we often nurture these old painful beliefs that we created at a young age without updating them. We update everything else around us to control our world. We update our clothes, support systems, homes, families, and values, yet we hold onto these old beliefs that continue to feed feelings that no longer benefit us.

Common Distortions

When we have beliefs that no longer work for us—beliefs about ourselves that distort our values and do not honor our truth—we call these one-sided feelings "distortions." Feelings that look for validation, negative or positive, draining our life force, are what we call in therapy "cognitive distortions." The most common of these distortions are:

- I'm unlovable.
- I'm not good enough.
- I'm undeserving.
- I'm a bad person.
- I'm stupid.
- I'm boring.

- I'm ugly.
- I'm worthless.
- Life must be fair.
- I'm abnormal.
- I must be competent.
- I must be loved.
- The world is dangerous.
- People are not to be trusted.

Distortions are the main thoughts that Fear provides for us to listen to, and it compels us to maintain and relegate these in order to keep the old uncomfortable feelings fresh and alive. Fear looks to the past for any information that will support these beliefs. Then it tries to convince us that the continuation of this feeling is the only possibility of truth for us in the future, and most importantly, that this Fear will continue to be our only truth.

Think of your own life and your own beliefs. Do any of the distortions resonate with you? It may be that small voice that talks to you when you want or desire more in your life. Or maybe they yell and fill your mind at night when sleep evades you, keeping you awake as you go through worst-case scenarios.

Known as cognitive distortions, these are the ways our mind convinces us of something that isn't true, telling us things that sound rational and accurate. We then go through life looking for information that will support our feelings but not logic, looking to support a feeling topic of Fear. Our minds are very good at finding "feeling" information. These inaccurate thoughts and feelings are then used to reinforce our negative thinking or emotions. Our minds will search for reinforcement of these feelings constantly until our thoughts are locked into a hamster wheel of distortion.

Here's an example:

> *In the past, I was unable to graduate from high school. I had a difficult time and was constantly filled with Anxiety; I could not go to school. Now I replay this information over and over. I*

rehearse the information and reinforce my feeling in an attempt to soothe myself and find an answer. My feelings and my worry tell me that I'm stupid, that I'm not good enough, that I will not succeed. I didn't succeed in the past, and this means I never will in the future. Sadly, I end up feeling as though there is no reason why I should try. The last time I tried, I failed, so I am sure to fail again. There is no way I can learn or overcome my feelings. If I try, I will just be making up stuff and lying to myself. I will not be able to succeed and move forward. I will always be the same. The future is written in stone. I know the future. It is and will be a repeat of my past.

In fact, it almost feels as though there is no future. There is only the past. Fear tells me I should not try. I cannot succeed. I am forever stuck, unable to move forward. I keep listening to my failures; I must listen to this Fear. I must run away from trying anything new in order to be safe. I must continue to listen to these thoughts yelling at me.

But, what about attempting to try something new? Maybe I can gather some new information. I may find out that I can learn, I may find out that I can succeed; I may find out that I can move forward, that the future is not the same as the past.

No, this is not true. That is not what Fear says. I should listen to Fear. It tells me I will get hurt, I will feel bad, that I am stupid. I need to continue to feed it and nurture it and keep safe here in my cave. I'm so filled with Anxiety, this must mean I need to run away from trying; I must listen to Fear, I must not try anything new.

NO!

Fear wants to keep you hostage to a history that no longer exists. It wants you to support it, and only it. As we work together, you will learn how Anxiety is not Fear, how Anxiety is the gatekeeper to Fear. Anxiety is here to ring the bells, sound the warning, and wave the flags, anything to get your attention. It wants you to stop Fear from devouring your life and your energy. It wants to help you listen to your thoughts and notice your opportunities, not Fear's feelings. Anxiety is with you to offer you an opportunity to examine the facts and the information from both sides, not to follow the bad feeling trail, feeding it, nurturing it, and keeping it alive long past its due date.

So many people say, "I felt afraid, I felt scared, I felt stupid, I felt worthless. Thus, I am my feelings and nothing more. My feelings rule my mind and my body."

For goodness' sake, NO!

Believing you are your feelings is a classic distorted thinking pattern. For example, "I feel lazy, so I must be lazy," or "I feel stupid, so I must be stupid." Feelings are not the same thing as who we are. Feelings are created by our thoughts. Our bodies experience our thoughts as chemicals emanating through a synaptic framework which becomes feelings within our body.

We have a thought—a thought is not something solid, unlike a spleen or a lung. A thought is a release of chemicals. The chemicals are released into the body. The body recognizes these chemicals and experiences them as a feeling. The chemicals can be anger, grief, joy, excitement, or worry. Our bodies' feelings start out as chemical thoughts creating a neural firing in our brains. Then the body sends that information back up to the brain, where we recognize those feelings as emotions.

It is a wonderful and beautiful loop of information, but that information is not us. It is information. We are so much more. We take that information and decide how and what we want to do with the data. That information is what we can then use, but it is not a person. We, the person, observe the knowledge and the thoughts. We, the person, notice how we are feeling and what we are thinking. We, the person, are the observer, the gatherer, the soul.

We are not a bunch of chemicals being released.

We are so much more.

You are not alone, if you would like ways to address your thoughts, look for the *Hello Anxiety* workbook or journal to guide you along through your process.

MIRACLE TWO

CHAPTER FIVE

TIMING AND SO MUCH MORE

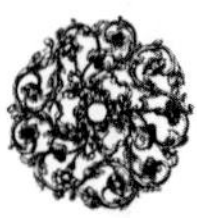

I am the Light Divine. I am Love. I am Will. I am Fixed Design.

—Alice Bailey

When the emergency crew arrived, they burst through the front door and raced up the stairs. My husband was still on the phone with 911. He had rolled me onto my side per their directions in the hopes of helping me not aspirate on the fluids coming out of my body.

My husband was relieved and yet terrified as the paramedics tried to assess the situation and decide what I was reacting to and why. My body was on the bed, foam emitting from my mouth, hard massive convulsions radiating through me. Not pretty television convulsions, but massive body distorting convulsions that left black, blue, yellow, and purple bruises all over my neck and body, wrenching me into misshaped forms as my husband frantically attempted to update the medics and have them give me oxygen. Suddenly it became evident that I was crashing. They grabbed my body, carried me down the stairs, where they strapped me onto a transfer board. They forcibly moved my husband out of the way as they began giving me CPR. I had completely stopped breathing. I had no pulse. I was blocked. The embolism stopped its progression when my heart decided to stop beating, stop contracting. No blood was able to move, and no oxygen was entering my system. They raced to the ambulance and took off toward the hospital, leaving my husband to gather himself and get to the emergency room.

When he burst into the hospital and found me, they had used electrical shock in an attempt to get my heart back online. There were fifteen doctors around, all yelling and screaming out instructions. The room was in organized chaos. People were strapping me into machines, working on bringing me back into the room with them, screaming out orders, pushing on my body, shoving needles into my arms as they worked to find any signs of life. But the embolism was still blocking me, and I went into cardiac arrest once again. The young doctor on call refused to let me go. He aggressively continued with my treatment pumping my body full of TPA, a massive amount of medication to break up clots.

Because I had recently gone through surgery, blood began to gush and seep out of my body in every direction and opening. Soaking through blankets, creating a dark crimson pool around me. The doctors soon became more concerned that I would bleed out and die from loss of blood than the clot.

Thankfully, I was fighting, and things began to move. I was able to get oxygen through my lungs with the help of respirators and breathing tubes. The heart started to beat, but the rate was extremely erratic. It was moving from twenty beats per minute to 240 beats per minute. My blood pressure was all over the map, almost nonexistent and then suddenly going so high there was fear of increasing damage to the veins and heart.

They pulled me off the TPA. I was hooked up to every machine possible. The noise was deafening when combined with the team working to bring me back. My husband was trying to answer questions, keep up with the movements of the treatment team, stay present, and make sure they did not stop the work of attempting to rescue me. His focus was only on the team maintaining their efforts to direct me back to this world.

My body was fighting. They could see me fighting. They knew I was still in there, trying to be in the room, to get back. My will and my soul were not going to let go. They would not give up, they did not stop, but my energy was so massive and erratic, they had to prevent it from draining my strength and me from working so hard. They decided to put me into therapeutic hypothermia—a frozen coma—to surround me with tubes of freezing water and run it through and around my body, lowering down my core body temperature.

During the cardiac arrest, my blood wasn't flowing to the organs in the body. The doctors discussed how my brain might not have received enough blood to continue functioning. This is why many people don't recover after experiencing cardiac arrest. The lack of blood flow can cause lasting damage to the brain. The person may never be able to regain consciousness. Lowering the body temperature right away after cardiac arrest can reduce brain damage. Lowering my temperature was raising the chances that I would survive.

I was in a coma for almost three days, frozen until I stabilized enough to begin the slow process of bringing me back to life. Like being in the cave, the process of reset needed to be slow and steady.

The paramedics at the fire department later told my husband that they had just returned from a call. If my heart had stopped twenty minutes earlier, they would have been delayed. The timing was perfect for them to respond. The traffic was light, allowing them to reach the emergency room and staff in record time. The staff was ready for my arrival, and the doctor was young and aggressive. Other doctors may have relinquished my fate to God rather than their dexterous hands. Everything lined up for the amazing treatment I was to receive.

Life seems like random events, yet the design and synchronicity of that day reminds me of something larger. The unfolding of events was uncanny, filling and pulling each person who surrounded us toward their life cord of purpose, tangling our energies in a musical symphony of energy and connection. A prevalent energy that keeps us tethered—tethered to each other, tethered to this world. It surpasses death. It is called Love.

Allowing is part of what Anxiety opens up for each of us: allowing the universe, God, life, destiny to unfold and provide options for us—options to grasp a new path without past preconceived notions. Guiding us toward our life and the beauty available for each of us.

It was a synchronistic harnessing of a crazy miracle.

CHAPTER SIX

BRAIN GAMES

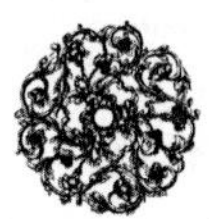

You've been criticizing yourself for years and it hasn't worked. Try approving of yourself and see what happens.
—Louise Hay, *You Can Heal Your Life*

My chest hurt; I felt my heart racing, but I knew I was more than an erratic beep of a machine, more than feelings, more than illness. I decided to be more. I experienced no doubt within as I reached to change my situation. Distortions had tried to beat me down and attack me like a saber-tooth tiger, but I held on to life. This was a battle I was familiar with, one that I had undergone once before.

As we go through life, awareness of how and when we create our own difficulties becomes essential. As a therapist, most of my clients are aware that logic is no longer moving them forward. Instead, they "feel" something that doesn't make sense or doesn't work for them in the same way it did in the past. They notice that they're not experiencing a sense of control, that they are off their road, their heart hurts. They feel negative emotions such as Anxiety, depression, sadness, shame, or overwhelm prevailing within their existence trying to knock them down. The feeling of Fear planted in their brain is now directing their future.

Remember, we are not our feelings, we only have feelings. Therefore, we have to learn to be more than our feelings. One of the first things I work with my clients on is recognizing their distorted thinking patterns. I have observed that each one of us typically plays with one or two distorted thinking processes. I call these the "games our brain plays."

Once we recognize these distorted brain games, we can name them, label them, and address them. If you don't know that you are playing a game, you will be unaware of the rules or unaware that there is a stop sign. So long as you're unaware that you are playing with distorted thinking patterns, you will not stop. You will blow right past the alarm bells, flags, and stop signs.

Beginning to notice when you are adding to your difficulties is imperative. Each game creates problems in our lives. Recognition of the game Fear is having you play allows you an opportunity to manage what you are thinking and, in turn, how you are feeling.

Games Our Brain Plays

Here is a list of common games or distorted thinking patterns I discuss with clients. Notice if any of these ring true for you.

1. All-Or-Nothing Thinking. *I faltered in my interview, so there is no way I will get the job.* This is an example of "black or white" or polarized thinking. This pattern occurs when we look at things in black-and-white categories. The person only sees things in absolutes—if they missed one thing, they must fail at all things. Thus, growth and enjoyment of imperfections are not possible.

2. Overgeneralization. *I am a horrible student and should quit school because I got a bad grade.* You view a single adverse event as a never-ending pattern of defeat. With this type of overgeneralization thinking, you take the failure of one specific task and generalize it to yourself and your identity. If something terrible happens just once, you expect it to happen over and over again.

3. Mental Filter. *My leg hurts so I can't enjoy anything about this day.* This game occurs when one dwells on the negatives and ignores the positives. A person who engages in filtering their thoughts magnifies the negative details while filtering out the positive aspects of a situation. The person cannot think about the friends who come to visit them, the laughter they have shared, and the love they are experiencing. All they focus on is the pain in their leg. They rehearse this feeling and look to find reinforcement from others.

4. Discounting Positives. *Yeah, my college diploma was just luck.* Those with this distortion pattern insist their positive qualities are not valid and disregard their successes and strengths while focusing instead on what they consider to be their weaknesses and failures.

5. Jumping to Conclusions. This distortion is when you jump to conclusions that are not warranted by the facts.

> **A. Mind-Reading.** *They never waved at me. They think I am horrible.* You assume what people are thinking and that they are reacting negatively to you. For example, a person may conclude that someone thinks badly about them but doesn't bother to determine if they are correct.
>
> **B. Fortune-Telling.** *Why bother trying for that job? It will not go well.* This common distortion is when we assume the worst will occur by predicting that things will turn out badly. For example, a person may anticipate that things will turn out badly and feel convinced that their prediction is already an established fact.

6. Magnification or Minimization. *What if my headache is a tumor?* Similar to all-or-nothing thinking, this distortion blows things way out of proportion or shrinks them. When a person engages in magnification or catastrophizing, you expect disaster to strike. Contrary to this, you may inappropriately shrink or minimize the magnitude of significant events until they appear tiny.

7. Emotional Reasoning. *I feel like an idiot, so I must be one.* Emotional reasoning is when your emotions take over your thinking entirely, blotting out all rationality and logic, and thus, you look to reinforce reasoning from your feelings. This distortion can be summed up by the statement, "If I feel that way, it must be true." Whatever a person is feeling is now believed to be automatically and unconditionally true.

8. Setting-The-Bar-Too-High Thinking. *If I don't get an A on every test, I'm doomed to be nothing.* This distortion is when we set the bar so high that we, in effect, set ourselves up to fail. Perfection is often thought to be average rather than exceptional. For example, I have to win every tennis match, or I'll be worthless.

9. "Should" Statements. *I really should exercise. I shouldn't be so lazy.* "Should" "shouldn't," "must," "ought," and "have to" statements are a list of ironclad rules about how we think people are to behave. Those who break the rules make the "should" person angry. They also find themselves feeling guilty when they violate their own rules. People believe they are trying to motivate themselves with shoulds and shouldn'ts, yet they end up punishing themselves, which ironically is the opposite of encouraging.

10. Labeling. *I'm a loser because I didn't win the card game.* Instead of describing an error in the context of a specific situation, a person will attach an unhealthy universal label to themselves or others. When someone else's behavior rubs a labeling person the wrong way—without bothering to understand any context around why they did or didn't do something—they may label them a jerk or hurtful.

11. Self-Blame. *We were late to the show and caused everyone to have a terrible time. If only I had pushed to be on time, this would not have happened.* You blame yourself for something you weren't entirely responsible for. This person believes that everything others do or say is some kind of direct, personal reaction to them. They take things personally, even when something is not about them. A person engaging in self-blame may see themselves as responsible for everyone's feelings and most everything.

12. Other-Blame. *Stop making me feel bad about myself!* Instead of self-blame, you blame others and overlook ways you contributed to the problem. When a person engages in blaming, they hold other people responsible for their emotional pain. They may see others as controlling their lives and feelings. However, nobody can "make" you feel any particular way—only we have control over our own emotions and emotional reactions. No one else has that control.

13. Fairness. *Jonny didn't have the red lights on his drive, it is not fair it took me more time.* People feel resentful because they think they know what is fair, but when others don't agree with them, they get stuck. People who go through life judging its "fairness" will often feel resentful, angry, and even hopeless because life isn't fair.

14. Always Being Right. *If they don't see I'm right, then to hell with them.* People who have this distortion will continually put others on trial to prove that their own opinions and actions are the absolute correct ones. To a person engaging in "always being right," being wrong is unthinkable—they will go to any length to demonstrate their rightness. Being right often is more important than the feelings of others, even loved ones.

These types of schemas and core beliefs amplify our stress response. They put one into fight, flight, or freeze, causing the body to increase its chemical Fear response, flooding it with cortisol and overloading the adrenal glands. The more these thoughts and cognitive distortions are used, the more your body responds with hormones and overworks the sympathetic nervous system. The threat is now within, and the body responds.

Stop and increase your awareness. Listen to the games inside your head. What is the Fear topic you are playing with? Notice when you are playing a one-sided game. It's easy because Anxiety will be with you in your body. Anxiety is asking you to take notice of the stop sign in front of you. Anxiety is your bell, your whistle, and your ability to know when these distortions are being played in your head. You can decide to blow past the sign into danger or stop and choose a different route.

Chronic stress and experiencing stressors over a prolonged period of time is the danger ahead, not the action Fear is stopping you from engaging in. The stress of non-action will result in a long-term drain on the body. As the autonomic nervous system continues to trigger physical reactions, it causes wear and tear on the body. It's not so much what chronic stress does to the nervous system but what continuous activation of the nervous system does to other bodily systems that becomes problematic.

I now found myself in the hospital heart monitors beeping—in many ways similar to a situation I had encountered in high school where I searched and actively decided to move toward my destination of choice. Choices open up a feeling of control. I knew this. For elusive control to be within our grip, we must work on our patterns of thought to be an expression of life. Increase our active choices rather than the stagnate ones Fear wants us to continually feed. Without doing so, our system starts to experience problems, and the body follows—when your old friend Anxiety is present know the tiger is attacking from within.

Fear is breaking down the body.

Self-Quiz

Look at the following list and decide which ones you often find yourself believing, the ones that will pull at you and cause difficulties. Know that other people will not hold your same expectations and concerns, which can cause more challenges for you in the future.

Common Irrational Core Beliefs

1. The world must be fair. People who don't act fairly must act fairly, are incredibly stupid, and should be blamed or punished.
2. I must be loved or approved of by almost all others who are significant to me.
3. I must be thoroughly competent, adequate, and achieving to be worthwhile.
4. It's awful and terrible when things are not the way I want them to be.
5. There isn't much I can do about my feelings because they are caused by what happens to me.
6. If something is dangerous, I should be worried.
7. It's easier to avoid responsibilities and life's difficulties.
8. I'm dependent on others and need someone stronger than me to rely upon.
9. My past history mainly causes my feelings and behaviors.
10. I must become very upset over someone else's problems and disturbances. This is especially true if I care about that person.
11. There is a right/perfect solution to almost all problems, and it is awful not to find it.

We are here to guide you. Take a Brain Games self-quiz at www.HelloAnixety.net and become aware of the games that may have you trapped.

MIRACLE THREE

CHAPTER SEVEN

GO AWAY, GO AWAY, GO AWAY

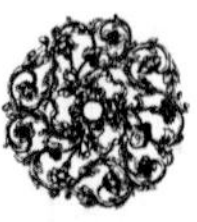

Physician, heal thyself.

—Luke 4:23 (KJV)

Her warm hand clasped mine, worried and yet relieved to be at the doctor's office. A door suddenly closed. Antiseptic wafted through the room as the cold, sterile table beneath me held my small body at attention. The posters on the wall were unmemorable, and the room was small. My mom and I were waiting for the doctor to come in, for him to tell me he would be able to do something.

I must have been about nine or ten years old when I came down with warts. I had them on my knee. At first, there was just one, then suddenly there were three. Before I knew it, I had a colony spreading all over, starting to move down as they claimed more territory on my leg. Small, powerless, not able to do much more than follow the rules, I was now in elementary school. I had to change schools—move from my friends, move into third grade, move into a new school district away from the familiar. Chaotic unknown movement that now contained warts!

Our classroom was set up in pods, a concept of the seventies, desks arranged in patterns aligned with the windows at our backs. Each pod or section confronted us with a different challenge. One was cursive writing, one was reading, one was multiplication tables, and then came the fun areas: baking, chemistry, building, drawing, and music. Like a video game, each challenge must be mastered to receive the rewards and enter the world of the fun exploratory pods. One had to pass through the deadly challenges and overcome the obstacles. You had to pass the reading, writing, and arithmetic. Let the horrific battle begin.

While most of the pods were easy for me to master, I had one monster that flattened my soul and ate my confidence each week: the multiplication pod. This dreaded pod was a recording that asked different multiplication problems—3 x 5, 8 x 6, 4 x 9, etc. Sitting with our backs to the wall, massive headphones on our ears, we would write down the answers and then wait for the results. The teacher would call out like an Emmy Award announcer which of the children could move forward and which of the children had to remain. Who would redo the battle once again?

Each week we would do the pods, and the teacher would announce who had passed and who could move on to the class. For whatever reason, I could not get through the multiplication section. Week after week, I had to repeat this portion. Each week the teacher would boldly announce I had once again failed. Soon, I was the only kid in the class who could not participate in the other activities. Whispers would echo around me as the rest of the class watched me sit and listen to the math pod, taking the test, certain I was destined to fail, while they baked, drew, built, and created.

All year I was excluded. I never passed that damn test.

I felt rejected, stupid, alone. No one would talk to me. No one would play with me. My world was small and dreary. Then suddenly, like an opening in the sky filled with dark clouds, a wonderful thing happened: an audition listing for a production at the local high school. They were doing *The Sound of Music.* The flyer announced, "Looking for children of all ages to audition for parts in our production."

I auditioned and was chosen to be part of the production. Suddenly I had people who would play and talk to me. We were a family. We worked together and bonded in our pretend family struggles. I was cast as a Von Trapp family member, Marta. The director would carry me around on his shoulders during rehearsals.

The kids at the high school were BIG. Cigarette smoke filled the halls, and loud music could be heard as it echoed, reverberating off the walls. They wore jeans and T-shirts, something I did not wear. They laughed with me, not at me. But most importantly, they liked me. It was amazing!

I started to feel special inside and free to express who I was or who I may want to be, a child with so much family to play and be with. On stage, I could pretend. I could memorize lines without any problem. I worked hard and loved each minute of it. The doubt, like dark clouds, began to fade inside.

Recently, I heard a story by Wayne Dyer where he was talking about a kahuna. A kahuna is a Hawaiian healer, priest, sorcerer, shaman, one who has the ability to heal. When Mr. Dyer asked him, "How do you become a kahuna?" The answer was, "You are raised to have no doubt." What a strange yet wonderful concept to encompass your life.

Doubt is the precursor to fear. Doubt only grows one thing: Fear. Doubt allows for hesitation and negative thought. Like a seed, it takes root, firmly planting itself inside. Faith is the opposite of doubt.

To have no doubt is powerful. When our faith in ourselves is clear and strong, we find we can create our truth to match. We can overcome and change our bodies. We can move mountains. According to Matthew 17:20, nothing shall be impossible to you. To be raised with no doubt is unimaginable to me. How can you go through life and feel confident, sure, and surrounded by nothing other than safety in your own mind? Where in this world can you experience this? How can we find that today?

I understand this concept and the power behind faith in yourself and a life without doubt. Anxiety is trying to push you away from doubt and doubt in yourself. Unbeknownst to me, I found the power of faith the day my doctor examined me and my warts.

The swinging door ushered in the doctor and his exam. He peered with a scope. He tapped on the knee. He watched my reflexes. His long fingers came to rest on his chin as he looked deep into my eyes.

"This is something that can be corrected. This is something that can go away, but it will take some work. Are you willing to do the work?"

"Yes, I will do the work."

I'm thinking he will pull out some magical cream that I will apply, or possibly the cure will be an extended process that requires me to come to multiple visits.

Fixing me with his eyes, filled with knowledge and surrounded by time and age, he stated, "Every night you will need to tap each wart ten times and tell it to go away, go away, go away. You will need to do this ten times—not nine, not eight, but ten times. You will need to say this three times. Each one, each wart—ten times three: ten taps, ten statements of three. Every night. Do you understand? Only if you do this every single night will the warts disappear."

"Yes, sir, I will."

"Do you promise?"

"Yes, I promise."

"Good, I'll see you back here in four weeks."

No doubt, full of confidence in his knowledge and in his direction, I would tap each wart, every night. And every night, I would state three repetitions of *go away* ten times. Like a religious practice filled with ritual, I would tap. I wanted to make him proud of me. I did not want to fail him or myself. Night after night, I spent much time and focus on my task, twenty-three warts in total all over my knee. Twenty-three growths I attacked with precision and belief. I was good to my word. I was thorough. I did not miss one wart. Each one got the same amount of attention and time.

Four weeks later, I met with the doctor again.

The warts were gone.

No Doubt.

CHAPTER EIGHT

THE POWER OF FEAR

My goal is not to be better than anyone else, but to be better than I used to be.

—Dr. Wayne Dyer

Pulsating like a sound frequency, a deep bass moving through our bodies, Fear radiates through us as a constant interference within, attempting to push us off our path. It eats at our energy, removes us from our life course, and tells us it is keeping us safe. But Fear does not inform us that it is keeping us from living. Instead, it consumes the exploration and curiosity that each of us has been gifted and, like a black hole, eats at our life energy, growing ever more powerful.

Our gift is the ability to decide with our free will what we prefer, what we like or did not like about our experiences, and that of which we want to explore. This gift, the gift of free will, is something we all deserve and have received through grace, not through earning. The free will to explore and decide what is aligned with our values, to reach and experience more of what our values point us toward. Each organ in our body knows this and tries to get us to listen and to hear the danger of not stepping into life experiences. They use Anxiety to talk for them, to message us that we are off course. And if we fail to respond, they become overwhelmed and begin to wither.

Both the sympathetic and parasympathetic nervous systems become alerted to the powerful interactions within our immune system. These systems allow the body to modulate stress reactions. When the system is thrown into overdrive, the body becomes exhausted. The body can only stay under high stress for a short period before the immune system begins to degrade and shut down.

The heart, the stomach, the brain, the nervous system, the lungs, the bowels, and the immune system are subject to stress changes and their ability to respond healthily. Remember that each organ in our body is trying to get us to listen and hear the danger, the danger of cowering in our cave, of not stepping into our lives, of running from a tiger that does not exist, of activating stress changes and thus activating our invisible superpower, Anxiety.

Our stomach and bowels are part of the mind-body-gut connection. Most of our "feel good" neurotransmitters are created within the gut. Thus, our stomachs require extra protection to ensure the stability of mood and homeostasis. Because of this, our intestines have a tight barrier to protect the body from (most) food-related bacteria. We know that stress and constant Fear cause inflammatory actions, making the intestinal barrier weaker and allowing gut bacteria to enter the body. Although most of these bacteria are easily taken care of by the immune system and do not make us sick, the constant low need for inflammatory action can lead to chronic problems such as our gut nerves being more sensitive, causing changes in our stomach microbiota, changing how quickly food moves through the gut and/or changing how our immune system responds to food and stress. Remember about our cave-dwelling ancestors and how our bodies try to protect us.

We instinctively know to listen to our gut. There are times in our lives when we listen to that small direction inside—the one that does not make sense, the one that has not gathered validating information to support our feelings. Our gut directs us to this resonating message within our hearts. We recognize the message is there yet, sadly, often we ignore the information. We understand that there is something we need to walk away from or into. Something we need to do differently, but we only hear Fear. Fear tells us to run from life, so we listen to Fear and run from life, from our gift, and the experiences that our body craves. We mishear the messages our body and soul are dictating over and over again. Yet Anxiety is there, watching over us as a gatekeeper. Anxiety is not Fear. We have mistaken it to be the same as Fear. So, when Anxiety is attempting to get our attention, we push it away. We despise it.

Anxiety actually wants us to step into life, wants us to not run from experiences or our gifts. It is trying its very best to redirect us to run from the misinformation and doubt that Fear is creating. Attempting to correct the misperception and direction that Fear continues to push us toward, Anxiety works hard to get our attention. But we shut it down.

When someone perceives a situation as challenging, threatening, or uncontrollable, the brain initiates a cascade of events involving the hypothalamic-pituitary-adrenal axis, which is the primary driver of the endocrine stress response. When individuals suffer from chronic pain, we know how they respond to the injury can make the difference. Individuals who are fearful of pain and re-injury and seek only a physical cause and cure for the damage generally have a harder time recovering. Muscle tension and muscle atrophy are common due to the body's disuse, all promoting chronic, stress-related musculoskeletal conditions. This ultimately increases the production of glucocorticoid hormones, including cortisol; we often refer to them as "stress hormones."

Remember, when your body thinks you are in a place of threat, it will respond as though it needs to protect you. Actively working on correcting any misinformation is up to you and, strangely enough, your superpower, Anxiety. If you constantly tell your body to feel threatened, constantly look for ways to reinforce knowledge about stressful feelings, you will spiral. If you choose to feed the Fear, you will drain your body with your mind. If you put your faith in Fear, you place your belief in only that which is negative. You now have faith in evil instead of good (Florence Scovle Shinn, 2021).

But know that Anxiety is with you. It is there, attempting to get your attention. Anxiety is trying to push you away from doubt, toward your gift, not the other way around. Not from faith. Not from the beauty of even the smallest of experiences. That is Fear.

Hear the danger and run away from doubt.

Listen to your superpower and run, run, run into your life.

CHAPTER NINE

QUARANTINE

When I was a child, I spake as a child, I understood as a child, I thought as a child: but when I became a man, I put away childish things.

—1 Corinthians 13:11 (KJV)

Where were you when you were told to shelter in place? Schools shut down. Offices shut down. Businesses shut down. Everyone needed a time-out. Similar to the JFK assassination and 9/11 terrorist attack, the world stood back in silence, stricken by change. But now the Earth joined in and became very upset. Telling all of us to stop, sit at home to think about what we want, where we place our energies, and how we want to be–what truly makes us happy?

Prior to the 2020 COVID pandemic, students complained about going to school, adults disliked their work. Yet people avoided trying something new, choosing instead to keep doing that which made them unhappy. Some people wanted more time to themselves. Less to do. Less pollution. Their families close. Well, as they say, be careful what you wish for.

For some people, this time was an opportunity. They chose to view this time as meaningful, using it to meditate, grow, and ponder who they are. For others, it was a time of grief and loss, work, and recognition that life was fragile, learning we could not stop the onslaught of a nonliving entity. People grew, and people died. The distance and disconnect magnified the loss. The grief grew each day with each lost life. It was as though we were in a world war without the war. Grief and love walked hand in hand, and love was there, holding us together as it attempted to direct this war rather than have hate fill us with Fear.

It was a time, though, to spotlight what was working for us and what was not. How were our relationships with our family, with our kids, with our friends? Did we want to continue the pressure of work? Did we like our jobs? Who was important to us? Who reached out? Who did not? Did we want more people in our lives? Did our lives feel full? How were our days and our mood while we sat with ourselves? Did we like ourselves? How bored would we become before we would find new ways to explore?

The first few weeks were crazy. Some people went immediately into Fear and control, their internal mantra, "The world will harm me, and I will be alone." For others, it felt like a long snow day away from school. Then reality started to set in. Our world was changing, and people began to notice that their thoughts about controlling the world around us were an illusion. All the things we normally tried to control were gone. We began to see we only have ourselves and our feelings to control.

Feelings are something people in the United States want everyone to agree on. You have to agree with what I am feeling. People want others to feel the way they do: "I feel this way, so you should too." Notice the distorted thinking pattern we just encountered, which, of course, causes so many patterns to be revealed. The "world war's" attempt to use love as a means to change our thinking about human beings, and our love of the Earth, began to crumble. Rather than gathering together to attack a common enemy, as we have done in the past, the country used people's feelings of Fear of conspiracy, Fear of competition, Fear of change, or Fear of nonsupport to muddle the waters. Rather than attacking the virus, we attacked each other. Love began to shutter and be forgotten. All of this caused Anxiety to rise and my pause at work to suddenly implode as it came to a screeching halt.

At our house for the first few weeks, we played games, did puzzles, and colored a vast picture with a never-ending design. We all worked at finding a structure for our day. For those with Anxiety, a sense of structure is very important. It gives an illusion of control. We work in a familiar pattern that we know and are able to find comfort in that pattern. I worked with my clients to look for ways to provide a sense of structure. What was their daily life before? How much time did they spend socializing, being creative, working, engaging in meaningful activities, pursuing a sense of purpose, exercising, and doing physical behaviors? I worked to remind them of the importance of reaching for social interactions, physical experiences, and creative outlets. We explored ways to find a sense of accomplishment, meaning, purpose, and ability. We worked our way toward a routine and found opportunities to experience new ways to explore things they had in the past, but now had to reinvent. These aspects of structure and consistency were needed to move forward. COVID created new challenges, and each challenge we encounter allowed us time to restructure and rework old beliefs.

Whether it is a pandemic or some other upheaval, it is important to ask ourselves, "How do I fill my life when someone else or something else has removed my norm or my sense of control?" Questioning ourselves often leads us back to a place of growth and love. We notice what we haven't said to someone, what is important to us, and how to ask and give to ourselves. We walk away from the pattern that Fear has built. The old patterns shift as we step into something completely new and different. Aim to allow gratitude and openness to guide you rather than our nemesis, Fear.

In the past during times of crisis, we, as a collective, have stepped away from power and Fear into love and concern. During crisis, our humanity called us to help neighbors. We played music, shared talents, donated food, clothing, or supplies. We wrote hope and love on signs, rocks, and together, we bonded in our understanding of how much we valued each other. We became an online society, a video discussion group, a computer team. We had to adapt because our world could not agree on how to eradicate the virus, so we had to decide on how to live with it.

Fear would not allow us to change too far or too fast. Love may have attempted to pushed us into a different place, yet when we began to feel our discomfort, we moved and pushed against the uncomfortable feeling. I saw as people let feelings dictate their actions. Fear told them, "Don't consider something totally different. It is uncomfortable and scary." Fear told us that if we do this, things will change, and change is scary—a change in our thoughts about ourselves and our possibilities. Instead, Fear said put your faith in me, not hope. Put your faith in Fear, not courage. Put your faith in Fear, not love.

In the United States, our businesses failed, our economy held on, our unemployment went up by 15 percent, and our death rate rose to one person every fifteen seconds. Yet we would not embrace a place of united resolve. Instead, we rebelled with Fear in our hearts and grasped at the old norm rather than reaching for something new.

But the world pushed us to remain in disruption, to move into discomfort. I often say to my clients that the unfamiliar is uncomfortable, but the more we stay there, the more familiar it becomes, the more we adapt, the more comfort we find. This place of a "new normal" allows us to update our childhood thinking of ourselves.

My clients asked me about my take on the virus. Why did this happen, and what was the meaning behind this experience? While understanding and possible meaning will hopefully come with time, I saw this as an opportunity to understand our values and embrace what is important. It was an opportunity to reevaluate our lives and ask ourselves these questions:

- How do we value connection?
- How are we to benefit, grow, and learn to support each other and ourselves with the time we are given?
- What is it that we need?
- What is it that we want?
- In what ways is Fear detrimental to our lives?
- What do we miss?
- What do we deserve?
- What is our relationship with God, Spirit, the world, nature, the Universe (whichever word you use), and how has the love within us been given a time to grow?
- How do we foster love within ourselves?

Notice your inner voice as you answer these questions. We begin to hear it pointing us toward connection, the world, and love. It points us toward what is working. Notice how Fear is disconnecting.

This lower consciousness, a consciousness that is based on competition, is what we as children experience. Fear breeds competition. We remember the concepts our children believed, the things they decided before they learned the truth. As they grew, they learned, they incorporated an understanding of social interaction and kindness. Unfortunately, most children do not find this as they grow. They start moving toward survival. Straying away from the concepts of love and acceptance, they grappled with the Fears created to satisfy their own consciousness and reality. Think of those middle school years: Children say things they shouldn't say. They react in ways that have no perspective. In this lower competitive consciousness, they often do not see and are unable to experience empathy or understand outside of their own self. Lower consciousness reiterates for the mentally young that survival is the meaning of life. It clouds the truth of connection and acceptance.

If I tell the truth, I will be punished. I cannot be the outsider, so I need to create an outsider; I need to join in even when I know it is not okay or hurtful. I must be part of the group at all costs. Lower consciousness.

Maybe you were told you did not deserve to be you. Maybe you were told that you were and would be judged, or you were told you were not enough. And the sad part is, you were told these things by those you trusted and those you loved. Those who were in authority said you had to climb and struggle for compassion. Even those who did not want us to think or hear these messages may have added to our misinformation, for we were only children. We had no way to understand other than lower survival consciousness. This lower consciousness story is the story we have been given time to update, time to listen to with the compassionate voice within.

We are now coming out of childhood, and we have been given an opportunity to work toward truth. Our truth is that we are loved, we deserve kindness, there is enough, and you are enough. We are known as Children of God, and now we can move into adult higher consciousness, a place where those we trusted had old patterns, thoughts, and beliefs—incorrect thoughts. Now is our time to embrace awareness. To correct our truth and know with full belief that love is the energy that powers us and moves us forward. It is a love for others and, most importantly, love for ourselves, faith in ourselves, compassion, and kindness. Now is the time to put away childish things, for it is the spark of a soul filled with love that ignites each of us.

We can work on our faith and belief in ourselves and the world. If we have been created in the image of God, then we have been created perfect in our imperfections: we are enough; we are to be cared for and loved. When we respect ourselves, others, and the world, we understand that life is not about Fear, survival, or competition. It is about cooperation, love, and inclusion.

Cooperation is a piece of learning we can take from the pandemic—cooperation with the Earth, cooperation with each other, cooperation with ourselves. Many will fight this and prefer to live in Fear. They will spread this Fear and attack those who are willing to move in the direction of cooperation and inclusion. This can be seen in the aftermath of the pandemic as Americans began to reach for inclusion and cooperation. The term, "BIPOC," meaning "Black, Indigenous, and People of Color," became part of our lexicon. This illustrated the American ideal of inclusion and cooperation while embracing concepts of equal protection, medical care, and human recognition. And the good news is, love is strong. Love, aligned with our values, will prevail. Love ties all of us together rather than pulls us apart.

That which draws us together makes us stronger; Fear will attempt to weaken our world with war, divide and push us apart.

CHAPTER TEN

ASK FOR THE COOKIE

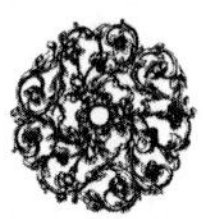

You miss 100 percent of the shots you don't take.
—Wayne Gretzky

I know what they are thinking about me and the situation. I know what is going to happen. It is pointless. I'm doomed. This won't work.

I often find clients use mind-reading or fortune-telling brain games and distortions. They tell me, "I know what will happen," or "I know what others are thinking." When I ask them if the person actually said that to them, or if others shared what they were thinking with them, the answer, invariably, is "No."

Of course, no one has a crystal ball to see into the future, and no one knows what someone else is thinking. I remind my clients it is truly none of your business what the other person is thinking. If clients were to walk around with their own thoughts being broadcast out into the world for all to hear—like a thought bubble hovering above their head displaying the inner machinations for all to see—it would be excruciating. Likewise, we are not entitled to other people's private thoughts. They are none of our business. On top of that, we have no idea what they have gone through, why they may be struggling, and what they are basing their thoughts on, unless they choose to share.

"Everyone will try to take things from me!"

"No one will support me!"

"I'm being judged and have failed."

Clients often fall into traps that tempt them to reach for old information and patterns. They believe the past magically dictates and grants them these powers. Walking in a trance of life, they move through automatic thoughts and behaviors, like a zombie eating their own self-esteem. They "know" because, in the past, "this" is what happened. They "know" because the past is the only thing that will happen again. They "know" because they saw it happen once before. They use these "knows" to assume what the future will hold, but even with enough known variables, no two situations can, or will, happen precisely the same every time. Unless you are performing a controlled experiment, distortions reside in the world of "knows," and people will use these knows as a basis for small, limited, "Groundhog Day" explanations of life. There are no other possibilities. The future is nonexistent.

For many people, asking for what they need or stating out loud what they want is taboo. In the past, this may have been met with disdain. They may have been ridiculed. They should know better. They may have been put down; they may have been told to think about all the people in the world who have less than them. How dare they ask for more or something for themselves. They need to be caretakers, to think about others. They need to be nonexistent to avoid hurt.

I use the following cookie story with these individuals: If you choose not to ask for a cookie because you have decided that the answer is no, you cannot have a cookie. You will experience your set of patterned decisions and denial.

If you deny yourself by not asking and you feel the answer is "no," then asking will not make it any worse. If you have braced for the no and you receive the no, nothing has changed, and you have not lost anything only gained what you expected. But if you have decided they will say no, then asking opens up the possibility of receiving a "yes." That is, if you ask in the first place. You only increase the possibility of better by asking. In other words, before you ask for something, don't assume the answer is already "no." Extending yourself by asking is the only way to check it out and insert the possibility of a "yes" into the equation.

Cookie Analogy

Warm and gooey, still soft from the oven's high temperature, they are just out of the oven, and they are calling to you. You can smell the warmth, homemade and promising, permeating the room with spice and sugar. Oh, they smell so wonderful, lined up along the baking tray, one dozen of your favorite freshly baked delights. They take you back to times in your past and fill your belly with warmth and memories. You gaze at the tray, stacked eight cookies long and three across. Filled with longing and desire, you look at the cookies. The cookies are your favorite dessert in the whole world, and you hope you will be offered one.

Option One: *You never ask. You say nothing. You never say out loud that you want a cookie. As a result, you do not end up with a cookie. Instead, you become hurt and upset. You leave feeling unloved and wounded. "They should have known I would want one. I mean, they are my favorite, and they were right there, delicately in front of me."*

You wanted a cookie. How could they be so thoughtless as not to offer you one? Those who assume others are not meeting their needs because others "should know" what they want typically are perfectionists. This lets me know that they are the ones who are projecting their own perfections and rules onto others. These individuals have been molded into someone who follows the rules of others, performs how they "should," and works to meet the made-up needs of everyone except their own self. To ask for their own needs to be met is either selfish or it means the other person does not care about or love them. They "should know what I need and what I want without me saying." They have assumed others should know this information because possibly they can intuit others' needs so well, and those around them ought to do the same for them. Or "I told them before, so they are choosing not to remember and be hurtful." When others are not retaining or are not showing they remember, individuals often feel as though it is a personal assault against them, and the one who doesn't remember or know that they want a cookie now is seen often as purposely failing the relationship rather than failing to maintain the client's personal unspoken standard of perfection.

Option Two: *You ask for a cookie. The person says, "Of course, please have a cookie." You feel good as you bite into the soft texture and feel the sweetness on your tongue. You are content and enjoy the wonderful feeling of the cookie melting in your mouth and filling your stomach with warm-cookie memories.*

Remember, if you have decided that the answer is "no," you will deny yourself by not asking. No one else said out loud that you could not have a cookie. Only you did in your own head. The reality is, you never asked for the warmth and memories to fill your being. You denied yourself. If you have decided they will say "no," then take responsibility for denying yourself. Do not place blame on someone else for this denial.

Option Three: *You ask for a cookie. The person says, "I'm sorry, but I made twelve cookies, and they are for twelve children. I am bringing them to the kids today. If I give one to you, one of the children will not get a cookie, and I don't want them to feel bad."*

You understand this, and it makes sense. You realize that you, too, don't want them to be denied. You remember being denied not feeling that connection to others and being alone. You remember feeling left out. You didn't like that and don't want someone else to feel that way. So, you feel good knowing you are doing a good thing by not taking a cookie. You know you can go and find your own cookie and experience the promise of freshly baked delights on your own terms.

Notice that asking for your needs to be met has allowed an opportunity for information to happen (curiosity). Not asking has shut this opportunity down and put you into a place of past information—Fear, Anxiety, and patterns. By denying the question, you end up being the person who continued the denial, not your friend. You presumed or intuited they were either neglecting your wants for a cookie or intentionally choosing to deny you the satisfaction of your favorite delicacy. You decided you knew everything about them and their lives and thus decided without asking for more information. You decided that they did not even think about you in the first place, not them.

In truth, neither of these are correct, but these "knows" of previous times clouded your judgment and limited your understanding of the current situation. Only when you stepped into asking for a cookie did the opportunity for a cookie increase. If you choose not to ask and you decide that the answer is "no," you will be denied. However, there is the possibility of "yes" if you ask. You already did not have a cookie before you asked, so even if the person cannot give you a cookie, you are no worse off than when you started by asking for a cookie. Yet you have received more information. Now you can experience understanding, acceptance, and possibly empathy.

So, when we are in a place of nurturing ourselves, in a place of self-care, we need to break old habits and ask for what we want. Using old brain games and distorted thinking stops new information and possible satisfaction. Remember, there may be a reason why the answer is "no," but we get clarity on the other individual's capacity to meet our needs. We gain the information we can use. We acquire the opportunity for a cookie and for the answer to be "yes." We can also care for ourselves by getting a cookie from someone else or making, or buying, our own.

When you know you want something, especially when you feel this something can help you, those around you who love you will take every opportunity to get you those cookies. But this action must include you. Not only will you get your cookies more frequently when asking rather than assuming others will offer but it helps people around you to know what types of cookies to give you and when you might need a cookie again in the future. We have the power within us to care for ourselves. Do not be the person who continues to deny yourself an opportunity.

Even in the movie *Groundhog Day,* the variable was the actions of the character continually changing. This affected the day until movement and needs were met.

So, ask for a cookie, and see what happens.

MIRACLE FOUR

CHAPTER ELEVEN

CORRECTING MISINFORMATION

All that we are is the result of what we have thought. The mind is everything. What we think we become.

—Buddha

No longer were the halls filled with stinky skunk smoke and cigarettes. Quiet and reserved, compared to the past, the 1980s—or the age of "Just Say No"—was in full swing.

As a junior in high school, I was still involved in the drama department and was now also active in flag and drum corps. Warm mannered and slightly frumpy, the drama teacher at our school was the same one that had welcomed me while I was lost and diminished in elementary school. The teacher was the same, but the students had definitely changed. Gone were the seventies of free love and expression. We were now in the eighties, pushing against the norms while fully embracing our definition of culture.

Being amid the angst of teen repression, I found myself surrounded by friends who enjoyed being as goofy as I did, no additives necessary. When I wasn't wearing my drum corps outfit for games, we modeled the Robin Williams *Mork & Mindy* outfit of jeans, a white T-shirt, and rainbow suspenders with lots of bling. Yes, we thoroughly enjoyed being the nerds, running through the halls singing songs, being young, and expressing our joy with no worry about what others thought. Screw the norms! Embrace ourselves.

I do remember it was during this time of my life that I took my first psychology class. Yes, I am one of those annoying people who said, "I know what I want to be when I grow up," and then actually did just that. I had decided I was either going to become a therapist or an actress. For me, they were basically the same thing. As an actress, you attempt to understand what the other person went through to make them who they are and then work to express this truth, perspective, and understanding to others. As a therapist, you work to empathize and understand what others went through to make them who they are today, what needs they did or did not receive. Allowing them to choose another possibility and deciding what their truth is while opening up to expressing it.

I had a plan. I was going to do therapy and perform this therapeutic connection while living and working on a sailboat. We would sail over the blue waves, feeling the air around us, connecting over and on the water, with the sun, the work, and each other together in the process. We would work through life's issues. I could connect with myself as I helped others do the same. Living simply, as I moved from place to place while exploring the world and people around me.

Though I had everyday worries and struggles, I was courageous when I was younger with my friends by my side; I felt minimal Anxiety. It seemed as though I could conquer the world. I was stepping boldly into life. Conquering my section of the world while surrounded by my support. With my wingmen by my side, I felt fearless. My friends were my protection. They offered not only friendship but also strength.

Betrayal, loss, uncertainty, and a beautiful mix of Anxiety and Fear arrived one day as my world came crashing down. Early in the morning, still half asleep, I called one of my parents, who had traveled away from home. But when the hotel phone was answered, the voice belonged to someone definitely other than my parent. Stunned, I handed the phone over to the parent by my side, the one at home.

It made no sense at the time. It was four o'clock in the morning where they were. What and who was that on the other end of the line? My mind swirled and then I pushed it aside. It wasn't until I got to school all the pieces began to fall into place. Suddenly, everything was upside down. My mind had a realization: everything would change. Panic!

My body reacted to a knowing that went through every bone within me. Heart pounding, each breath came fast and furious through me like a growing wave, a wave of panic. Tears streaming down my face, my legs ran automatically to the nearest cave: the bathroom. I wanted to crumple on the floor, the weight of my body holding me frozen in guilt and fear. Sobs burst out of my chest, stopped by denial. The aching within grew and exploded as my heart quivered, till one of my girlfriends arrived and surrounded me. Her arms filled with the support of strength I did not have as it moved into me from her. She was there, holding me tight, open and caring.

And then came the next shift. I got sick. Each stressful situation began to build. Fear held me close. It told me to back away from life and love and exploration, that safety was an illusion and life was dangerous. Remember when we are running from the tiger, and more and more stressors are added, our immunity suffers.

I had tried out for the play *Our Town,* and I was waiting to see what role I would get. I was at home in my blue-and-yellow-wallpapered bedroom with a full princess bed when misery started to slither in. The covers felt scratchy, and my body temperature rose rapidly. Red coloring creeped over my skin as I turned slowly into a crimson Violet Beauregard from *Willy Wonka* while my body temperature continued to rise. Becoming weaker and weaker, energy drained out of my body as confusion began to enter. At the time, toxic shock syndrome was the talk of the newspapers, and my mother was certain I would be its next victim. I didn't care what this was. I just wanted it to stop.

Smelling like disinfectant, riddled with noise and people, I remember walking into the emergency room. Hazy and surreal, the room swirled, the desk miles away from me. Like a dream, each step took me farther from my destination. As I reached toward the person far away, suddenly I was on the floor. My body rebelling and fighting and trying to burn out the infection with a fire from inside. My temperature was so high that I could not walk and sustain consciousness. I passed out.

Everything else was a blur as they rushed me into the back and began triage. They hooked up machines and placed monitors on me, working to see if they could control the fire from within. No matter what they did, they could not bring down my temperature. They tried medications, fluids, and tests until they finally decided to place me on ice. Swathing me in cold, they set me on bags of ice wrapped in towels to lower the rising temperature as it crept higher and higher, 103 then 104, and still moving higher. The ice bags were placed under me, next to me, and on me. They continued to work on my body, freezing, shivering with cold, and the high temperature. I can still remember the cold racking through my frame and the tears streaming down my face, pleading with the staff to stop.

The ICU room was enclosed in windows, openings for the staff to monitor from a distance. I remember seeing the bank of windows and feeling my body cold, shaking uncontrollably as I looked out to the people on the other side. They had moved me onto ice blankets. Horrible, cold, ice-filled pallets were being used on my body as they tried to bring my temperature lower. I was so cold my teeth were chattering, my body cramping, as tears and pain emanated from all that was me. I could feel my muscles attempting to move away, deeper into my skin, away from the cold, inward toward warmth—my chest filling with pain as the unbearable cold seeped through my skin.

Suddenly, my body was convulsing either from my high temperature or from the ice blankets. I can't remember which anymore. Machines started to go haywire as the noise filled the room and flowed out to the hallway. The machines beeping and yapping, screaming outwardly about the pain I felt inside. The noise filled the staff and doctors with dread as it continued its screams of distress.

I clearly remember looking out the window and seeing the doctor talking to my mother. I could see the concern written all over the doctor's face and hers, and then the worst thing ever happened. Her face collapsed, and she looked like she wasn't going to be able to stand. Her entire body went limp, and her breathing stopped for a moment. The look was so dramatic and the Fear emanating from her was clear, I knew they were telling her I wasn't going to make it. It was like her world was coming to an end. That was when I decided "NO." No!! This was not happening, not like this. Fear, stress, confusion, nothing but me would make this decision. I was in control of me. I could see the beeping and yapping machines all around me. My heart rate was all over the place, up and down, fast and stopping, crazy, crazy pain and the hurt in my chest—the pain was so intense. I decided this had to stop. I had to stop this!

I focused on the machine that showed my heart rate and my breath. With each breath, my focus grew, and with each breath, I decided to make the beeping even and steady. My heart rate began to go down. The *beep, beep, beep* of the machine started to be a steady musical rhythm. I watched the numbers and breathed out the number that I wanted the device to say. I knew I could do this—and I don't know how I knew. I just knew I was in control of my own body no matter what. Each breath and each beep of the machine saw my heart continue to settle as it slowly began to beat more and more within a normal range.

The doctors came running in as my mother's face eased and became hopeful. No matter what they said or did, I would not remove my focus. I continued to make a game out of the beeping, having it slow and create a beat, a beat to a rhythm. I worked and breathed; I focused and listened to the machines' rhythm till the pain in my chest no longer burned, and my breath was slower and more manageable. The doctors all surrounded me, and the hopeful noise level in the room began to grow. My mother kept telling me to hold on. I was doing well. I could do this. A deep sense of calm came over me. An understanding that there is more in the world, and I would hug my family once again.

Lo and behold, I did end up having toxic shock syndrome (TSS). It so happened that a visiting specialist from the CDC was speaking on TSS at the hospital the day I passed out in the emergency room. They called him in after my mother kept yelling, "She has toxic shock. She has toxic shock!" And sure enough . . . I did have toxic shock. I was the thirteenth case registered in the United States. My fever came down, my entire body peeled from the high fever, and I was monitored for years afterward.

I remember the pain in my chest and the pain Fear painted on my mother's face to this day. In that moment I had faith in my superpower and used it to direct my full-on determination to stop Fear and listen to my Anxiety. I had been certain I would not die, for my Anxiety was there talking to me, directing me to take control of my own destiny. I never doubted it. It never even crossed my mind that I could not stop my erratic heart rate. While Fear tells us to control things outside of us—other people's emotions, their action, their thoughts—Anxiety knows we are only in control of ourselves. I was in control, and I knew it. There was a reason, a design to life. It was slowly presenting itself to me.

And once again, here I am, but this time it is my husband watching the machine beat its insane beat through the window. I'll need to remind him about high school.

It was a crazy miracle.

CHAPTER TWELVE

RECOGNIZE AND DISMANTLE

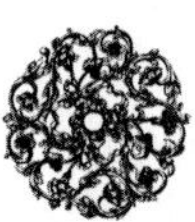

When awareness expands, events that seem random actually aren't. A larger purpose is trying to unfold through you.
—Deepak Chopra, *Spiritual Solutions: Answer's to Life's Greatest Challenges*

STOP! Easier said than done.

I often hear how a client is feeling miserable, and thinking positive thoughts feels too hard and stupid. "Okay, so don't. Instead, notice your thoughts." For me, I experienced an extreme situation that allowed me to understand I am not my feelings, I am not my thoughts—I am the director of these experiences. In the depth of this challenge was the voice of Anxiety, incessantly working on getting my attention. Like a wingman and a best friend, they encircled me and infused me with their caring.

Awareness of our thoughts is the beginning step in noticing how Anxiety is trying so hard to work for you and not against you. Upsetting emotions—worry, shame, anger, or depression, to name a few—are all flags your body uses to get your attention.

They are a means to help us notice when we are heading into danger. When there is a stop sign in front of us, we need to decide: do we want to continue down this path in the same way we have before? When I recognized the doctors had decided I would not make it, a big stop sign flew up in front of me. I made a decision. I would not rush forward into the same thoughts, the same feelings, the same disastrous situation.

You need to understand that these feelings are helping you recognize when you are engaged in a distorted thought, a distorted brain game. And it is awareness that is necessary for you to stop playing the distortion game and step into a new possibility. Once you know you are playing a game and what game your brain likes to play, you can begin to dismantle the thought, change the game, and utilize the anxious feeling as your red flag. Anxiety wants you to get out, stop, and change the game, like being unaware you are in a video game or a matrix. Wake up!

Having Anxiety is your red flag. Every time you feel it, stop. Ask yourself what you are thinking. What thoughts are going through your mind? What were you thinking before this happened? What do you want to be feeling? What would you rather be feeling at this moment? I guarantee if you feel Anxiety, then you are doing one of the mental distortions. Notice which game you are playing. Notice what the distorted thinking pattern is. Know you can change this pattern. Decide to change course. Decide not to blow through the stop sign into danger. Become aware.

Notice if you have been gaslighting yourself: "I don't deserve to have that."

Have you been saying one thing and doing another? "I don't want people to judge me, but I can judge them." Are you the hypocrite?

Reflect

The following is a process to help you dismantle these distortions based on the work of Byron Katie. In her method called

"The Work," she allows the individual to see their part in the distortion.

Working in conjunction with your therapist is advised. I have included a five-part reflection process that can assist you in recognizing your truth. This process may take some time, so do not rush yourself. If you want to delve deeper, look at the *Hello Anxiety* workbook to walk you through this process.

Remember, Fear wants you to find ways to validate and align with it. It is not having you step into courage, hope, or love. In order to create a continued balanced story, step into this process with openness. Check to see if your evidence is fact-based or feeling-based. Remember, you are looking for facts. Once you have the facts and information, you can then decide how you step into a feeling you prefer.

Distortions are a one-sided conversation. When our brain looks to find evidence that only supports one side, we get pulled away from our truth. Don't believe Fear, who tells you nothing will and can change. You can change. You can open yourself to new perspectives. Opening up to perspectives from a different viewpoint helps us to find our truth.

Use the following process as a beginning for rewiring your brain. Work to utilize the facts, not only feelings. This process can open you up to options. The option where both sides of information can permit you to move in a new direction away from the negative feelings of the past. By looking for evidence to support both sides—evidence for and evidence against your original thought—you allow for a two-sided conversation in your brain. The past, present, and future are all different times. None are the same. Always remember, if they were the same, they would have the same name. The past is to be used as a place for understanding, learning, and values. It is NOT to dictate future hurt, sadness, anger, shame. It is not here to subtract from your present moment. The past is here to direct us forward to a better future of opportunities.

Fear wants you to come up with facts to fit only the Fear

response. Anxiety wants you to turn it around, find out the facts, information, and then decide how you feel. By aligning the brain with the facts that represent both sides of our inner conversations, we can hope to find balance.

Work with a therapist until you get to your core belief. Find your new balanced story. Learn how to feel good, connected, not alone. Turn it around! Step into the process.

Reflection Process

Paragraph One

Start by writing out the upsetting thought that is playing over and over in your mind. Utilize these prompts to organize your thoughts:

- What did you want?
- What would you have preferred?
- What did you not get?

At the end, consolidate this into two sentences.
Example: Sam doesn't listen to me.

Paragraph Two

- Is this true? This can only be answered YES or NO.
- Be honest with yourself, be still, and find the answer.
- Can you absolutely know that this is true 100 percent of the time?
- How do you react when you believe this thought? (Notice the feelings, sensations, and behaviors that arise when you consider this thought.)

Paragraph Three

- What about this points to a value I hold?
  Example: I'm afraid Sam doesn't care.

- What is it that I value?
- What images do you see, past or future, and what emotions or sensations arise as you think on these aspects?
- When I think this, I feel . . .
- How have I stepped into this value?
- What can I do to express this value?

Paragraph Four

Work on noticing the brain game that is being used by your brain.

List the **facts**, not feelings, from the previous paragraphs that others and myself are showing this value.

Facts/Evidence I am showing this value:

A.
B.
C.
D.

Facts/Evidence others are showing this value:

A.
B.
C.
D.

I Have Learned

Go back to your original story, ask yourself:

- What does this mean about me and my values?
- What have I learned?

Example: I value respect. I want Sam to respect me, but I often don't show respect by listening to him/her or myself.

Rehearse this factual truth, over and over again.

- List out what your feeling is now on a scale from 0–100.

For a deeper understanding of this process and more opportunities to address your beliefs, look for the *Hello Anxiety* workbook. Here, we will walk you through the process of uncovering the emotions that may be holding you hostage.

CHAPTER THIRTEEN

CONCERNS OF THE HEART

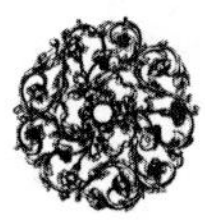

The wound is the place where the light enters you.

—Rumi

MIRACLE FIVE—*Oops, just kidding*

I loved those warm summer nights filled with the scent of the sweet evening wisteria that flowed outside in the yard. Picnic tables placed end to end covered with newspaper, and flowers spilling out of canning jars, welcomed our friends to our home, called the "free house" because it was so inexpensive. Small and cozy, the house embraced us with a measly $380 per month mortgage payment, allowing us to throw large Friday-night supper parties feeding whoever was able to come by. Big parties with a low country boil poured out on the table—shrimp, potatoes, sausage, and corn served hot, steaming and weeping with flavor. Fresh bread from the farmer's market with butter and goat cheese smeared along its jagged edges filled the table. Beer and drinks flowed as the conversation met the alcohol and continued into the night. Those occasions were wonderful and seeped into who we were, permeated into the flowers and the grass, the walls, and days.

The backdrop to this was my repetitive stressful job. We were constantly pushed to bring in money, watched by management to ensure we made our quotas which increased each time we succeeded. I was allowed one picture in the office. I chose a black-and-white Ansel Adams print of a large tree, its branches reaching for the sky. A desk, a chair, and a door signified that I was an adult. I was making my own money, but the stress began to build. I had some good relationships within the office and opportunities to share. There were people I enjoyed and some with whom relationships were strained yet doable. It was a job. It was a job I was thankful for, and it allowed me to purchase our first home. The "free house"–yellow and small, a two-bedroom, one-bath home with a large backyard–spilled over with laughter and friendship. It became our refuge.

We lived in an older area that had not stood up well to time. On one side of our home was an eighty-year-old widower, frail and personable. On the other side, a young urban couple who sadly were not friendly. My future husband and I cared not about the diminished area but that the people we lived around were accepting, kind, and showed care for their homes and love for their families.

Though the neighborhood was crumbling, we loved this house. It had a white picket fence out front surrounding a large magnolia tree reaching for the sky. Like my Ansel Adams print, the tree was old and graceful, filling a huge part of the yard. And our home had a fountain in the living room. Yes, a fountain in the living room. Stained glass windows, a large backyard, a shed, and a workshop—all so cozy and quirky. The woman who lived there before us was an older southern woman. When we walked through the yard of our soon-to-be first home, she went through each of the plants in the yard, explaining their history and names, like children she was sad to part with: "This one came from my grandmother's garden. It is known as a rose of Sharon. This one I remember from when I was a child; I was able to graft this out of my aunt's garden."

During these magical days, my boyfriend became my fiancé. Of course, the proposal is a whole other story for a different time, but we were happy and looking forward to the celebration. We knew each other, and we understood each other's needs. Acknowledging and respecting our differences, while recognizing these experiences in our life had allowed us to be unique and connected to this world. It was a wonderful and happy moment in our lives.

I was at work, achieving goals and creating new and different ways to reach our customers—making calls, sending letters, reaching out. Then suddenly, I felt my heart rate increase, and my breath raced. My arms became numb, and I lost the ability to focus on what I was doing. Pale and scared, I reached out to the staff. I worked for a doctor who took my blood pressure. It was through the roof.

Paramedics and sirens filled the office halls. Once the ambulance arrived, they strapped me onto the gurney and raced off to the nearest hospital. My heart rate was all over the place. It concerned the hospital doctors. No one seemed to know what was happening. They monitored me until my blood pressure dropped and normalcy stepped in. They didn't know what to think. The staff kept me there for a few hours before finally releasing me.

This happened well before cell phones, so my fiancé did not fully know what was occurring. The doctor called, and we met at the house once I was released. I seemed okay. The doctors were confused but assured me I was all right. They wanted me to seek a specialist who would monitor my heart. I was told that I was okay, sent home, and asked to follow up later. They were going to observe me.

Two days later, I had another episode. The ambulance was called, tests were run. My heart was erratic, but no information as to why. They called in the specialist, who said they wanted me to wear an ambulatory EKG machine. This way, they could see when and possibly why my heart continued to go "offline" and recommend a solution from their diagnosis. I wore the leads for forty-eight hours and never experienced the same concerns while attached to the mechanism.

Eventually, I was diagnosed with pulmonary atrial tachycardia (PAT). The symptoms include palpitations from a rapid heart rate, dizziness, and weakness. The doctor put me on beta-blockers, which helped keep my heart steady and regular. I was okay. I had to eliminate caffeine—Oh my GOD, coffee! Once again, this was before decaf coffee was a thing and I had to monitor and watch myself. Ugh . . . what?

I thought nothing more of it and continued to move forward. We got married and had an amazing wedding experience. As I worked, I moved into training employees, then eventually up to headquarters. It was then that I decided it was time to step into my dreams. I had been walking the life expected of me, not the one I knew I wanted. Finally deciding to live my truth, I went back to school for my master's in psychology.

Feeling blessed that I found a program where I could pursue schooling on the weekends, I continued to work while at school. I took out loans—lots and lots of loans—and was able to pay for my expenses, as I had to cut my work time by half and then eventually stopped working altogether as I pursued my dream. While becoming a therapist, they set you up for NO MONEY. You must work at your practicum for free, then your internship for free, then a thousand hours for free, then you can get your associate license and charge reduced fees, and then after three years, you can get paid. Ah, the world of psychotherapy—"the dream."

During this time, when I was studying abnormal psychology (one of the best courses in psych), I suddenly had an epiphany. As a student, you read through each of the concerns and diagnoses of psychological issues, and you begin to realize, "Oh my gosh, I do that!" Strangely enough, this is okay, as each problem is a part of our experience and is relatable. We all experience some aspect of each of these diagnoses, but the key is that they are not overtaking our lives, not overwhelming our values. Diagnosable concerns are disruptive problems that engulf our way of life and cause problems connecting with others. It is a diagnosable issue when the problem affecting your life ends up controlling you rather than you controlling yourself. You can't move forward. You feel stuck. This is when it becomes a problem.

I was reading about Anxiety when I suddenly realized, "Oh my gosh! I had panic attacks." This is why they didn't find anything wrong with my body or system. This is why the doctor decided to put me on beta-blockers. He was trying to eliminate the initial response for panic that I experienced when I felt that loss of control. After that, it all began to make sense: marriage, divorce, family, and commitment—my history of loss and lies with my own family—each of these affected my ability to trust, to allow someone else into my life who could possibly wreak havoc. Yes, each of us knows divorce exists, but we blissfully go along, never thinking it will happen to our family. What if it happened to me?

Before my marriage, my mind had been running through worst-case scenarios. Was I setting myself up? Was I walking into the same mistake my parents walked into? Were marriage and love something that lasted? Was I being made a fool of, opening myself up to failure? Would my future husband leave me, lie to me, hurt me, make me feel loss and abandonment? I had been worried, concerned, anxious. I was experiencing a stop sign and misread the information. Information was telling me to stop the comparison of past and future. Stop the Fear that wanted me to subtract from my life. Stop and move forward.

Then it hit me. I had been experiencing ANXIETY! Abandonment issues!

I had panic attacks. It all made sense.

CHAPTER FOURTEEN

JUSTIFICATION

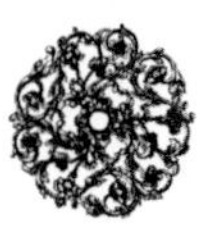

If you're trying to justify something, you're trying to escape from something you do not want to admit to.

—Teal Swan

Perfectionism is a curse. It is a self-imposed created problem where people often sadly imagine that perfect is obtainable. Perfection is not attainable; it is continually moving and changing. God is perfect. Man is not. I am here to tell you the hard truth, though it is challenging to hear. You will experience self-assured failure if you try to obtain perfection. No justification will make this different.

The other side of the perfection coin is imperfection. Imperfection is the one thing we humans have in common and this side of the coin opens us up to finding connection. No matter our hair color, language, religion, skin color, or education, no matter what we do or do not have in common, there is one common aspect that allows us to be human:

IMPERFECTION.

Yet, strangely enough, we attempt to hide our imperfections from one another, despite the fact that we share this common trait. We are all imperfect and can connect within this knowledge. It is this knowledge that allows us to bond, learn, and strengthen our ties to one another. When we share our foibles, others see us as human beings (fallible humans just like them). They relax and decide if they want to join you and share an authentic experience. These imperfect people are the ones we like to be around, the ones we don't have to be better for, the ones that enjoy us for ourselves, and the people for whom we do not have to put on the "pretend mask" of an imposter. The ones we can laugh and share our misadventures with. The ones who we know are not going to judge us, for they, too, are imperfect in their own way, and they own it!

Sharing my own story with others, including my imperfections and process, has made me more human and approachable as a therapist. Understanding my values and limitations, I have learned to accept that values are guidelines put into play when we try, whether we fail or not. Working on our values and how we align with those values helps us stay on course. This learning opens us to walk into the difficult times we encounter, challenging us to clarify ourselves as we continue to step into our principles while sharing our imperfections and trials with others.

When we begin to believe others are judging us, we are in danger of judging them. As Wayne Dyer states, "When you judge another, you do not define them, you define yourself." Are we trying to escape something we do not want to admit is against our own truth? We often become the culprit of our own demise, causing our downfall into a place of inequity when we fail to recognize and identify our own fallibility and challenges. How does one, as a perfectionist, find a way to encourage ourselves to be nonjudgmental? How can I reach for nonjudgment of myself when challenged and decide instead to reach for curiosity? That is the work we do within psychotherapy.

Curiosity is a cure for Fear and the opposite of judgment. If we are curious and ask questions about what is true, what is not valid, what is fact, what is fiction, what could be an outcome rather than the one Fear has dictated, we open ourselves up to connection and discover what fits within our tenets. When we own our lack of understanding and express a desire to learn, this sense of curiosity allows us to break free from Fear and enter a place of possibility. Possibility opens us up to new truths and to ourselves. It opens us up to nonjudgment of ourselves and others, while Fear keeps us captive and shut away. Whenever we give way to Fear, we feed our own monster. Growing and never satisfied, it is a monster that we willingly carry around, nurture, care for, and keep alive.

Judging a person or one moment in time with no substantial and logical information feeds the monster. Yet when we open ourselves up to the digestion of multiple pieces of data, suddenly, we allow ourselves to be provided the best information. Think of people or an experience as a vaccine. If we were to make a vaccine and only try it on one person, one time, would we feel safe and secure with the information available only from this one source and event? Would you feel confident and comfortable basing all future outcomes from this one person's vaccine outcome? Of course not! Yet this is what we do every day to ourselves. We have a one-time experience, and Fear tells us that it will be the same outcome EVERY TIME. Fear also wants us to believe others will not learn from their past experiences. So, in this example, if the vaccine didn't work, no one would use this information to change and grow. Here are examples of this type of thinking:

> *Well, I went to the grocery store and had a panic attack, so the grocery store must have magical qualities that cause me to have panic attacks. I have decided I will base all of my information on this one event, even though I have not experienced panic at the grocery store in the past.*

Or,

> *I was driving on the highway, and that part of the road must be filled with magic panic-making materials. I know every time I venture there, I will feel the same thing even*

though I have driven across the country without experiencing this panic before.

Or how about when it hasn't even happened?

I almost passed out, so now I can't do that anymore because if I do, then I definitely will pass out in the future.

Using this feeling-driven logic inhibits a future for ourselves. There is only a past and a one-time-only past at that.

I see people trying to logic their way into why they should not become curious and see if their premise is true (notice the distorted thinking in this statement). Fear holds them tight, telling them, "Maybe you should believe something that is not fact and then go and base your life on it."

People find themselves judging their actions and other people's behaviors based on the rules they have created from their experiences. They go into a thought pattern where they justify for themselves that, *If this is the way I choose to think, then everyone else will be thinking like me and judging the situation and themselves based on my rules.* So, when we hear people state "they should" or "I should," therapists know we are into distorted thinking patterns with self-imposed rules.

For example:

"This happened to me, so it will happen to everyone."
"I must be perfect, and so should others."
"I have to be the best, and so should others."
"If I'm not perfect and the best, others will see that and judge me for my faults."
"My experience is the only experience anyone will have."
"What happened is only about me and nothing and no one else."

These rules are often harmful and make no sense, and in

them, we find we have created a judgment—one that we have placed not only upon ourselves but the world. Notice if we turn around the statements, the statement becomes us judging everyone else. We have drawn a line in the sand.

> *"Everyone is exactly like me."*
> *"Everyone should be perfect."*
> *"Everyone else also must be their best if I am my best.*
> *"Others are judging me for my faults, so I should judge them."*
> *"No one will have a different experience than mine."*
> *"I should be the focus of everyone."*

Our brain then looks for a way to validate this feeling of our judgment. Our brains are diligent and efficient as employees at a company looking to authenticate the information our boss has decided they want. Like a topic the boss has placed on a table for everyone to prove correct, our brains go into distorted thought patterns to find this proof. Proof that maybe they can read someone's thoughts. "I know what they are thinking. I know what they will do." Then the boss tells them to search for validation of this thought and this topic, and so off they go.

Yes, yes, they may know that it makes no sense, but they feel like it is true. Suddenly, they are nurturing their inner monster: the one who wants their emotions to rule their lives, particularly the negative ones. If you allow your feelings to lead your life, you tell your body you want no part of control. You are taking the stance that the mind and soul do not matter—instead, only the body and the feelings from your body matter. Remember, thoughts come from the mind and create feelings in the body. What and how you think allows these feelings to be produced.

If I were to tell you I would take you up in a plane and throw you out, would you feel Fear, scared, excited, exhilarated? If you loved skydiving and were a skydiver, and I told you I would take you up in a plane and throw you out, you would be excited and thrilled. If you are afraid of heights or concerned with not having control, and I said I'm going to throw you out, you would be scared and terrified.

It is the way you think about the activity that allows you to feel. Whatever your thought, that thought produces the feeling, even with loss and death. For example, if you lose someone you are very close to and who means a lot to you, the feelings of love and loss are significant. Yet if you hear about the loss of a coworker's cousin whom you did not know, your feelings are muted and less. It is how we think about the situation or how we think about the people that cause us to feel. The feelings are not in charge. The way we have chosen to think about them creates our pathway.

To say I am not in charge of my thoughts means you have relinquished control of your mind to practice some predesigned feeling. You are thus acknowledging you are walking around in a trance—a place of automatic thoughts and reactions. Yet, if you are alive, you have the ability to think. You can choose to see the rain as refreshing or as dismal. It is your choice. To say otherwise is a copout. To say, "I can't choose my thoughts," indicates that you are a robot of Fear, that you have relinquished yourself to Fear. You have chosen Fear to rule your life. If this is where you are, then the fight is straightforward. You need to work hard, and with a support person, with a trained therapist, you need to remind yourself about what is versus what you feel. What are the facts rather than the feelings? Your thoughts have become automatic, causing a physiological and chemical change in the body.

Individuals may look to validate a topic and experience with no information, no logic, in order to justify their thoughts. They have yet to recognize that they are the ones trying to escape from the self-judgment within. Instead, they have drawn their line in the sand.

It is the same thing as ringing a bell and having the dog salivate. Your body has returned to the past and rehearsed the same event, emotion, and reaction. But it is up to you to regain control.

You have the power to heal the hurt, the loss, the trauma, and you do not need to do this alone. Support is available, but only you can do the work.

Suppose your problems were to be gone suddenly. How would you feel? If they were never to have happened, how would you think? Now notice how often you spend your time feeding this past monster. How often do you nurture the same old feeling, the same old thoughts, the same repetitive actions that have led you nowhere but to a place of feeling powerless? Are you willing to stop nurturing the problem? Or do you genuinely wish to continue to feel the same emotional trauma where you are working to keep it alive? If it is in the past, notice how you and only you keep it alive with your thinking—no one else except you.

MIRACLE FIVE

CHAPTER FIFTEEN

CAR ACCIDENT

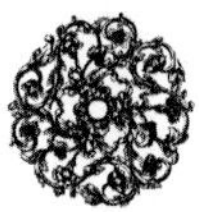

Our values are like points on a compass.

—Robert D. Zettle

It was a beautiful summer day as we drove down the road, the quiet surrounding me and my girlfriend as we piled the kids into the back of the car—car seats, bathing suits, snacks, bottles with juice, and water. My two boys were excited about us going to see Grandma. It was going to be so lovely to have another adult watch over them so we could sit and talk with each other. My girlfriend, whom I'll refer to as Elaine, and I hadn't seen each other in what felt like forever as the days and distance separated us, but not the feeling of connection.

When we arrived at Grandma's, the house smelled of warmth, with crisp, sizzling, smoky bacon on the stove pulling us forward. Fresh pancakes and the whirl of the fork as Grandma whipped the eggs into a frenzy of puffed perfection. Her language of love is food. Homemade pancakes, bacon, hot cocoa, and eggs filled the kitchen with their smells—the love of sizzling grease bubbling up like a conversation. The familiarity of comfort, chit-chat, and acceptance radiated out to us as we sat, talked, and digested our food. The food was filled with the love only a grandparent can bestow upon a breakfast.

Grandma had a large saltwater pool, blue and bright, with a lovely shallow section and depth at the other end. Then, of course, there was the obligatory kiddy pool on the side, where the warmth of the water made you wonder, sun or something else? We packed drinks, sandwiches, towels, toys, shampoo, and extra clothing. Off like explorers, we ventured into the open grasslands of the west.

Next to the pool was a playground filled with swings, rope climbs, and slides. The boys loved climbing, yelling, and going to the neighborhood tennis courts to look for lost tennis balls. We spent the day enjoying our time, laughing, and swimming. The sun slowly dipped toward the west as the evening rolled in. All too soon, it was time for us to pack up the kids and say our good-byes.

The boys were still little, walking and talking, but comforted by routine and the presence of their adults who watched over them like eagles to see that they did not step out of the nest. In keeping with our roles, we placed them in their car seats as we hugged Grandma good-bye.

My oldest was three years old, and my youngest was two. Sleep started to creep in as the boys ate their yogurt. Their eyes became heavy as they held onto the half-empty cups. Elaine and I talked and gabbed, settling into the day's refreshing and comfortable activities, exploring the past and enjoying the present. We were about eight miles from the house, passing a small store and the state prison, when suddenly an approaching car swerved into our oncoming lane. It happened so fast, I remember only having time to think, *Should I swerve and get hit on the side or take the impact head-on?*

Thankfully we were only doing about forty-five miles per hour, but the other car was coming at us much faster. My instinct was to stomp on the brakes and receive the hit head-on for fear the kids would take the brunt and impact on their side of the car. It was maybe two seconds, but it felt like time stopped and sped up all at once. Contracting my muscles, I stomped on the brakes. I braced myself on the steering wheel. Thank God for Saturns. These were the first cars to be made where the vehicle would crumple and break away. Rather than the entire car taking the impact, they made each Saturn so sections would respond to the impact and keep the rest of the car intact.

Then everything went flying. I was heading for the windshield. Elaine grabbed the dash and braced herself. Yogurt went everywhere—and I mean everywhere. The next thing I knew, we were in the middle of the street, and Elaine was gone.

I started to freak out. *Where the hell was she?* The windshield was intact but shattered. I swiveled behind me for the kids, and I caught a glimpse of her running down the street. She had jumped out of the car and was running toward the guy who had hit us. His car, smoking and leaking fluids, had come to a halt sideways in the street. It was crumpled. Yet as Elaine ran toward him, he fumbled for the keys throwing the car into action and took off. She was able to get his license number and the make of the vehicle as she turned back toward the rubble she had escaped. I started to reach for my babies as Elaine returned, yelling to me, "Don't remove them from the car seats!"

What?

As you might have gathered, Elaine had been trained to respond to a crisis, and her training had kicked in. She told me not to remove them from the car seats until the paramedics had arrived. If they had sustained any injuries, it was best to keep them immobilized, and the car seats would help with that. We removed the seats from the mangled car and put them onto the sidewalk near the store. People who had witnessed the accident or who had heard the sound came streaming onto the sidewalk. There was a lot of rumbling and mutterings about "This is not right!" or "This is not okay," "There were little kids in the car!"

Screaming sirens echoed among the homes and buildings. The sound filled the air as the police arrived, followed by an ambulance. They checked on the kids, and they looked us over. We were stunned and sore, but thankfully all in one piece, and the car seats had worked like a charm. The kids were just fine, not a bruise to be found. Yet time slowed again as it seemed forever before the tow truck arrived. Questions from the police swirled in our heads as we attempted to find calm and move toward our cave. The entire questioning period is a blur, but I clearly remember the crowd becoming more and more agitated. Apparently, the crowd knew who owned the car that had hit us. And boy, were they pissed! Finally, the police said they would have to leave to investigate and apprehend the assumed villain for fear, with the growing crowd, there was going to be a vigilante killing, agreeing to keep us updated as they moved forward with their investigations.

As the tow truck driver pulled us up in front of my house, we gently eased our sore bodies out of the truck to the front door. I held my babies close, smelling their scent and feeling the warmth of them as my girlfriend called my husband, who was overseas. Exhausted, we fell into bed, stunned that we were okay and still in shock from the blunt force of the accident. We were all right. We survived the tiger and were back in our cave.

Elaine and I woke up the next day with black and blue bruises growing and extending over our frames as the pain broadened deep within our bodies, but we were alive!

Frantically making his way back to us, my husband went to see the car. It was completely demolished: the engine was in the front seat, the front was basically missing, and the sides were crumpled beyond recognition. Yet, from the back . . . the car looked completely normal, wholly and strangely normal. So, as I look back, I am glad I made the decision to take the brunt force of the car head-on. If not for this decision, my kids may not have been okay. Focusing on my children being held safe in the car was the emphasis of my emotions and my decision. There was no Anxiety at that moment. It was not necessary. My thought process was accurate and aligned with my values. My core sense of truth and values was expressed.

It was a crazy miracle we survived.

CHAPTER SIXTEEN

THE TOPIC ON THE TABLE

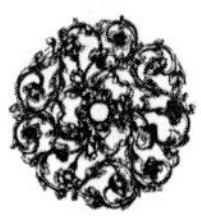

The greatest weapon against stress is our ability to choose one thought over another.

—Williams James

Bruised, sore, and running for our cave, we end up picking up the broken glass of our lives when we blow past our stop sign. Like people's misconception of what they are experiencing, the broken glass is what their Anxiety wants them to avoid. Like a plague attacking their system, they wish to eradicate this Anxiety problem, yet the "Anxiety problem" is trying to get them to stop. Stop beating themselves up, stop predicting the future, stop mindreading, stop terrorizing themselves, and stop, stop, STOP running away from their values. They don't understand this yet, and they focus on controlling things outside of themselves and stopping everything other than their thoughts. It takes quite a while for people to comprehend that this feeling is not a plague. Anxiety wants them to stop playing distorted brain games and align with their values. While they may understand logically that all of our feelings are necessary and needed, Anxiety is not on their list. So, I have devised a way to explain to them what and who Anxiety is.

Anxiety is almost always misconstrued as Fear, yet there is a difference between the two. When we have something to fear, we don't feel Anxiety. Instead, we feel Fear—only Fear because it is appropriate. Anxiety says, "Yes, listen to that Fear!" But, when our Fear tells us there's a saber-tooth tiger in the room that does not exist, our Anxiety comes online to help us.

"What the heck, don't listen to them; there is no saber-tooth tiger!"

When Fear is necessary and relevant to the situation, there is no need for Anxiety. As with the car accident, I aligned with my values. Yet when Fear is not aligned with our truth and values, Anxiety is there to help.

The Board Room

Imagine a classroom or a boardroom. It is extensive and impressive, with a long table surrounded by chairs in the middle of the room. Each chair is filled with a person or classmate, all of whom are looking onto the center of the table. Piles of books are on the table, and on the floor—books, laptops, phones, papers, pencils, and pens surround each person. You enter the room, and the manager asks you to climb onto the middle of the table and stand.

Leery and taken aback, you climb onto the table and take your place. The sound of scribbling is heard as the manager writes something on a piece of paper, a topic for the people to research. Like a big search engine primed to find anything they are asked to acquire, these people do not care about the subject. In fact, all the people around the table are here to obtain whatever the manager asks. They don't care about what they are searching for. Like a computer, they are supposed to find anything that authenticates the information the boss manager has asked. Anything at all that will assist in validating the topic placed in front of them, whether that is a question or thought.

Think about putting a search question on your home computer. Does your computer have a judgment about what you are searching for? No. It does what you ask. It finds anything you need to locate. If you want to find information on why dogs drink milk, it will find information about milk-drinking dogs. However, at this table, Fear is the boss manager, and it throws out the topic, "I will be alone."

The employees go crazy, pounding away on their computers, looking through the books of your life. These people are your memory, and the information of every thought and event you have encountered is at their fingertips. Details about your past and your life are just waiting for them to uncover. They hold every piece of data and every feeling you have ever had in their fingers. They begin researching every little detail they can possibly come up with, anything to support the premise that you will be alone forever!

It starts as a wave and builds momentum. Reverberating quietly, growing louder and louder, until the people around the table are screaming information at you, yelling about how you felt alone as a child. A cacophony of how you were misunderstood, how others did not accept you, how you are different, how no one truly knows who you are, how you feel you have no real friends, how every failed attempt has dictated your inability to succeed.

When they run out of information from the past, they start to make up future information. They take everything that happened or could have happened and tell you it will continue to happen. You will never be surrounded by those who care for you, you don't deserve the love you are looking for, and you will not achieve this goal of love. Even if it could happen, it won't happen in your future. You must see this. You must know they are correct. They pretend to see the future; in fact, they make up an entire world of pretend that hasn't even happened—yelling and screaming at you, overwhelming you with feelings as to why you will be alone. This one thought, this one possibility, they are only looking for any information or any justification to support this one premise.

Now, your best friend, who had gotten up from the table when you arrived to get a cup of tea, has returned. They come back to see this horrible debacle of yelling and screaming with you on the table, listening to all of this nonsense. They are horrified!

"Oh my gosh, what the heck?! This is so crazy."

They run over to the table and try to get your attention.

"Stop listening to this. This is not okay. Stop, STOP! This is so wrong. This horrible negative conversation is incorrect!"

But the voices are too loud, and your friend can't get your attention. In fact, you can't hear them over the yelling and screaming. Your friend knows you will not be able to discern their one voice from the other yelling employees. So, reaching across onto the table, grabbing onto your feet, they start pulling at you, trying to get you to get off the table, to get you to stop this flow of concern. Soon they are crawling onto the table, shaking your shoulders, attempting to get your attention, trying their hardest to get you to stop listening to this nonsense. But you are so engrossed and overwhelmed, even though you feel them tugging, you can't seem to disengage.

If they could only get you to move off the table, to have you stop the topic, stop the data, stop the onslaught! Your friend loves you and cares about you so much. As you become overwhelmed, your eyes are glassing over, and your body is frozen, listening to the noise. Your friend can't get your attention. They are so worried about you, and it seems as though there isn't anything they can do except finally tackle you and throw you onto the floor out of the room.

This is known as a full-on panic attack.

Your friend, your best friend, the one who will never, never, ever give up on you, the one who rescued you is Anxiety.

Anxiety cares about you so much they will take you down onto the floor rather than have you listen to the one-sided talk of FEAR.

BALANCED THOUGHT

What if things had been different, and the topic presented to you was a balanced question, such as, "Is it possible I may have love in my life?" Like a big search engine, each member at the table would investigate to find anything that supports this topic. Anything at all that will assist in uncovering information on the topic placed in front of them.

Pounding away on their computers, the employees begin looking through the books of your life, every piece of information, of every thought and event you have encountered at their fingertips. They begin delving into every little detail they can possibly come up with, anything to support the premise that you may not and that you may find love.

So now your friend Anxiety will shut up. Instead, they will sit down in the corner, allowing you to hear the pros and cons, the possibilities, the good and the bad, all of the information needed for you to decide what you want, how this aligns with your values, and what is in your best interest.

Your friend Anxiety is fine with both sides of the information being presented to you. Anxiety trusts you to listen and discern what is correct for you. Anxiety believes in you if you are given the opportunity to hear the good, the bad, a balanced conversation, and the possibilities. Anxiety trusts you will decide what allows your values to be pursued. But if you only hear a one-sided conversation, then no! An unbalanced conversation not in your best interest, and one that will overwhelm you? Heck no! Anxiety will not be happy.

What if the topic of thought is "positively" one-sided, like, "Everyone in the whole world will love me and only me." Once again, Anxiety will rear its head and say, "Whoa! Hold on, something about this is not okay; this is not in your best interest. This does not align with your values. This, my darling, is a one-sided conversation!" But a balanced conversation—evidence for and against, one that may bring understanding and compassion—with this information Anxiety believes in you and your ability to decide.

So strangely enough, Anxiety is here to help you. Anxiety is your inner superpower. In fact, it is your old friend who believes in you. Anxiety is here to keep you centered. Anxiety is here to let you know when Fear takes you off course from your truth. Your truth is Anxiety's primary goal. It wants you to step off the table, reach for other perspectives, and curiosity, and to stop the distorted brain games. It wants you to see when you have blown through the stop sign and warn you that you can get hurt. It wants you to find what your truth is and pursue that truth.

For more work on your topic and aligning with your superpower, head to www. HelloAnxiety.net and dig into the online course.

CHAPTER SEVENTEEN

WILL YOU MAKE ME CLUCK LIKE A CHICKEN?

It's not the mountain we conquer but ourselves.

—Edmund Hillary

I love hypnotherapy. It allows the client to reorganize their experience, take control, step into a new perspective, and write out their own new and updated belief system.

There are so many misconceptions about hypnotherapy. I start by explaining to clients what it is and why I find it so useful. The client directs where we will go, not me, and they come to their own conclusions. I am there to assure they are not alone, moving toward their best interest and reaching for their values.

Clinical hypnotherapy is not magic, and it is definitely not what you see on TV or in the movies. Allowing your brain to do what it already does every day of your life—quiet, focus, and work through the problem rather than ruminate—is why hypnotherapy works so well. I ask clients if they have ever been driving and gone into deep thought and suddenly arrived at their destination and did not remember how they got there. This is self-hypnosis. Even though they were not "aware," they did not run over people. They did not speed through stop signs. If a child had run out in the road, they would have shifted their focus and slammed on the breaks. Our brains use autopilot to wander through the world. We spend most of our time in a trance. In fact, studies have shown when we try to focus, our brains wander away constantly. Hypnotherapy harnesses this to our advantage. Even when we are focused inwardly, we are still aware of the outside world.

As our brains drop down into theta waves, the subconscious is allowed to open. We naturally move from beta to alpha to theta and then into deep sleep waves as we fall asleep. When we are between alpha and theta, and are still awake yet almost asleep, both parts of our brain align and begin to talk.

Our brains do this each evening, dropping down into a place of rest and rejuvenation. When you are about to fall asleep, and suddenly your brain opens up—your long-term memory brain, also known as the subconscious mind, opens up to the world. This is when we find ourselves wondering, *Did I finish that assignment? Did I take out the trash? Is the laundry still in the dryer?* This experience is expected as our subconscious mind switches on and our conscious mind turns off, often causing us to become stuck in our thinking, late at night. We utilize this during hypnotherapy: our ability to access all of our mind, both the conscious and subconscious. Your awareness and concentration are greater during hypnotherapy, and more of your brain is available for you to access information.

So, if you were about to fall asleep and a friend leaned over and quietly said, "Hey, cluck like a chicken!" You would open your eyes and say, "No!" This is how you would also respond to me if I suggested something outside of your value system. Now, if you had a desire to cluck like a chicken, you might, but that would be your decision and not mine.

Our conscious brain is the part of the brain that controls logic, reason, our executive functions. It is the latest part of the brain and the last part to form as we grow. This part of the brain is the part we use to work on self-control and cognitive flexibility. In fact, it doesn't fully form until our late twenties. Most scientist agree this happens around twenty-five to twenty-seven years old, if not later. It provides direction, a sense of self, and decision-making abilities.

Our subconscious brain is the older and more primitive section of the brain. This part houses our long-term memories and self-preserving aspects of brain function. It is the part that reviews and activates old feelings and automatic processes.

When we are using both areas, we can understand the past and its effect on us. We can clearly see the aspects that have brought us to this moment. We can activate reason and step into new patterns. We can align with our sense of truth and self. We are no longer acting rashly with no guidance system of logic and flexibility or being ruled by the muscle memories and old feelings that do not allow for a future. When all parts of the brain are online, we have a sense of understanding, an epiphany.

When only one part of the brain is directing, we become lost. We lose perspective and possibility, as our feelings of the past direct our future allowing only the past to be recreated. Or we do not learn from what we have experienced, and neglect to utilize this reasoning to enhance our future, such as what do we prefer, what do we not prefer?

Even though they may not have fully formed executive functions, children can connect with their creativity and can easily access what is in their best interest during hypnotherapy. In this realm, they, like adults, can experience understanding and receive it from within.

Clients with Anxiety are often trapped in feelings. Their feelings are directing their future rather than creativity and the information of perspective. They can only recreate the same feelings of what has already happened to them. They know that what they are feeling makes no sense, yet they follow it repetitively, doing the same behaviors over and over, amazed when the outcome is the same or grows more powerful. Doing the opposite of their behavior pattern and becoming creative is what Anxiety is asking them to pursue: run from the repetition of the behavior and thought, and become curious about the future and themselves, break away from the trance of the past.

Imagine a tug-of-war game going on in your brain. Some of the people involved represent your conscious brain—ten people looking for new opportunities on one side of a tug-of-war rope. Then there are the ninety people feeling the past who want to direct your future on the other side of the rope. In this tug-of-war game, the ten-person team most likely will not win.

When working with clinical hypnotherapy, you are activating both parts of the brain in unison—having all of your brainpower work together with both sections on the same side of the rope. All possibilities are opening up to you. All infinite possibilities are available to explore. If being stuck in negative feelings no longer serves you well, know this negative feeling is there to remind you, "Don't go this way!"

With hypnotherapy, we use this feeling power to direct us to the core of these issues and open up the past for understanding. We then combine the knowledge of new possibilities with this past and create something new, freezing the incident, allowing for non-permitted expression to be released—creating a safe space to process these options and a new direction. When we step into all of the brain talking and listening, we get clarity. A new thought is formed rather than the repetitive tape of the past, replacing old beliefs and patterns that are no longer useful or fitting.

Ian Cleary, psychotherapist and neuro-linguistic programming (NLP) hypnotherapist, said, "It is not enough to just stop Anxiety in any given moment, which is often people's focus. The wiring is still there and waiting to be triggered. We need to create competitive wiring. We need to create specific wiring of what we want to achieve, which is 'competitive wiring' to the problem. Without this, we loop endlessly in Anxiety with no neural pathway to take us forward" (Ian Cleary, 2015).

The new pathway is one of options—one of kindness, exploration, trust in self—the message Anxiety is looking for you to encounter. Clinical hypnotherapy allows the client to be self-aware, not unaware. It allows the client to make their own decisions, directions, and feelings rather than having others from the past decide how they feel and why, including their own past selves. It is empowering and self-directive. Offering the client an opportunity to align their feelings finally with their current thoughts. A new reality can be claimed, and your inner mountain can be climbed.

CHAPTER EIGHTEEN

CREATING MY REALITY

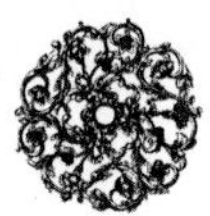

"Why are you afraid, you men of little faith?" Then He got up and rebuked the winds and the sea, and it became perfectly calm.

—Matthew 8:26 (NASB)

So many of the directed hypnotherapy tracks I found to use for myself were not what I was looking for. They all talked about the future of what would be, while what I was looking for was a knowing—knowing it already had occurred. I wanted to utilize my brain's want of using the past as an indicator for the present. If the past had already happened, I could step into my present: the feeling of faith—a deep sense of that which was authentic and that which would not and could not be shaken. A complete understanding to experience what had already been written. No doubt, only faith.

Matthew 17:20
And He said to them, "Because of the littleness of your faith; for truly I say to you, if you have faith the size of a mustard seed, you will say to this mountain, 'Move from here to there,' and it will move; and nothing will be impossible to you."

Knowing that I had conquered each challenge I encountered, and feeling that I was okay, became a daily meditation. Stepping into the reality of faith and knowing and creating my life allowed me to reach for what I knew was possible: no Fear—only certainty and expectation of desire. I knew that nothing was impossible. I had to believe and feel the type of faith that comes from looking back and seeing what had already happened and knowing it as truth. I had to experience the future as my past.

I could step into a new future of possibilities in the same way we look back in time at the party we attended and remember the laughter and fun we had, which allows us to reach for more parties. I needed to grow the neural connections of my brain and encounter my positive past so it would be my reality. Thus, creating a future with my newly desired positive feelings of my own creation. If my feelings could dictate the future, then my feelings could allow me to step into a new future. I needed to reach for positivity.

Contrary to this direction, people often choose to grow negativity. When they look back at a party, they may choose to remember looks or laughter as judgments about them, opting to create fear, justifying why they should not reach for opportunity or to keep them from venturing onto new opportunities. They look for anything that will back up this premise of judgment. *Did they look at me funny? Maybe they were talking about me? I will pull away and not enjoy those around me, so now I feel disconnected.*

Those who grow negative pathways now increase the feelings of judgment and being alone by judging themselves and others. You are growing your own negative pathways—no one else, just you all by yourself. No one else is thinking these thoughts for you. Only you are in charge of growing these pathways, watering the neural pathways of sadness, disconnection, and competition.

Yet when we choose the opposite by electing to grow positive neural pathways rather than negative ones, we open up our lives to a future with love and laughter. Knowing these pathways are a part of everyone's design in order for us to experience health and life, I began my own process of creating what I needed to feel and an ability to move toward certainty. I began to rehearse my own future truth.

Here is one of the self-guided meditations I created and used to open up possibilities as I rehearsed my truth:

Meditation: Embrace

Take in a slow breath.
Feel the release of the worries and stress of the day from the body with each exhale.
Beginning to feel relaxed and comfortable.
Thoughts are breathed out with each breath.
Only focus on the slow, gentle breath.
Listening to my voice.
Notice the natural rhythm of the body. One that allows relaxation even more.
The eyes relax.
The forehead relaxes.
The jaw relaxes.
The tongue drops gently to the bottom of the mouth.
The shoulders drop down.
The mind calms, allowing the experience of a miracle.
The body calms, the mind relaxes, and the real true self is revealed.
The dreams and desires are true.
Take time to visualize your feet.
Letting go of each toe and the stress.
First the big toe, then the second toe, the third toe, the fourth toe, and the pinky toe.
The tension fades away.
The mouth is not too moist, not too dry, but perfect and comfortable.
The legs let go; the belly softens, feeling the warmth in the heart, like the warmth of the sun.
The relaxation grows as the body begins to tingle.
There is a slow coherence that begins to grow between the heart and the mind.

It allows movement from the body into the space around self.
The heart and mind begin to beat as one.
Feel the draw upward to the divine above, where the truth of self and connection lie.
I hear my voice, soft and constant:
I am able to think greater than my consciousness and conditions.
A vision forms in this space.
The smells, the taste, the feelings begin to form.
Alive in this space, it becomes clearer, drawing me in.
Into the true me.
Falling in love with this vision, my body knows and loves it.
I walk right into this vision.
I notice the questions that begin to form.
What would it be like?
I notice the passion, the emotion, the intersection of truth.
I am in alignment with the divine.
Surrounded by the love that is within and around me.
Guided by love that sustains and grows, like the healthy cells in my body.
My body knows what it needs, and I listen and respond.
Divine love flows through every cell in my body.
I experience love and give thanks to every part of my body.
I know divine love is in every cell and atom.
I believe in my body and the divine to keep me strong.
It has healed me from within.
I am laughing.
I am healthy.
I am running and experiencing life to the fullest.
I feel truth.
Warmth and love surround me.
I am enjoying life.
I am with family.
I am surrounded by nature.
My mind, body, and spirit are in harmony.
Each cell in my body is healthy and filled with love.
They reproduce and fill my body.

Only that which is in my body's best interest is absorbed.
I have lived a long and healthy life.
I love taking care of myself.
Harmony and divine love interconnect us all, moving me with its warmth.
My skin is smooth, soft, and supple.
My body enjoys the healthy food it is offered.
I am digesting nutrients, feeding my cells and soul.
Divine love protects me and guides me.
I am and have been blessed with health.
All the cells in my body vibrate and generate health and harmony.
A deep feeling of love and gratitude for the workings of my body radiates through me.
Divine love has blessed me with the power to heal.
Divine love has blessed me with the power to have been healed.
I am surrounded by an environment of stability and alignment.
The more I relax, the healthier I grow.
I am in an environment of health and healing.
I focus my intention on the true me.
I feel and sense the true me in the here and now.
What is the first thing I did knowing the true me?
I feel it happening now.
I see it and feel it.
I have created a wonderful life for myself and my family.
I have attracted the divine into my life.
I am so happy in this amazing life.
The God of my understanding manifests miracles.
I am grateful for my miracles.
Grateful for the life I have.
Take in a slow breath.
Feel the release of the worries and stress of the day from the body with each exhale.
Feel relaxed and comfortable.
Each thought is breathed out with each breath.
Focus is on the slow, gentle breath.
Listening to my voice.

MIRACLE SIX

CHAPTER NINETEEN

MINDFULNESS

If you die before you die, do you die when you die?
—Jon Kabat-Zinn

Most people have no idea what mindfulness is. All they know is, *I tried it, and I'm not good at it*. Well, of course, almost nobody's good at it. But strangely, that is the point—noticing how we are not good at it and noticing what we are doing instead. Mindfulness is something we know everyone says we should do, yet we all ask why. What's the point?

The point is multifold. The first is to notice your thoughts, what type of ideas you are having, how you feel when you have those thoughts, and how often your brain meanders away from the present. The next is to train your brain to stay in the present and come back from the past or stop wandering into the future.

I often have clients express that their brains are supposed to be quiet and not be thinking about anything when they meditate. For goodness' sake, no. If you are not thinking about anything, you are dead. Being dead is not the point of mindfulness. It is the opposite. It is to notice what is going on in your head and become mindful of your thoughts. From there, you can build up to seeing what is driving those thoughts. You become mindful of how you can stay in the present and how you are in charge of these thoughts.

Knowing what and how to stay in the present is an entirely different way of knowing. By using mindfulness rather than being in the past, all you need to notice is when you're on automatic pilot, being pulled away from the present, and deciding to be better than your automatic pilot.

Our brain is so good at seeing things that are not there, and when it focuses on one aspect, it will not take in other important information. For example, it will overlook new and current information if it is focused on looking for information to prove the past. The "Selective Attention Test 2.0" video of white shirts passing a basketball is a beautiful way to demonstrate to others how we tune out information when we decide, "This is important." When we have been told to count the number of times those in a white shirt pass a basketball, the brain will decide this is important. Watch the video, notice what your brain takes in and how well you count the white shirts. Notice how your brain is not reliable. The information we take in is compromised through confirmation bias.

Staying in the present can help one notice when you are beginning to go into negative thinking. Thinking that everything is about you or that everything is against you will cause your body to break down. Stressful feelings about your belief of worthiness, including loss of hope or change, will damage your system. The cascade of stress to your system will cause your body to degrade. Science can now prove that real stress comes from our thinking. It is our perception of stress that decreases and degrades our telomeres and our bodies.

Telomeres are found at the end of our chromosomes and stop the deterioration of each chromosome. When our chromosomes degrade, we become ill and age. Thankfully, science has caught up with Mideastern thought. Elissa Epel and Elizabeth Blackburn from the National Academy of Sciences Lab have shown that telomeres' length makes a difference in our life expectancy and quality of life (Epel, E. S., Blackburn, E. H., Lin, J., Dhabhar, F. S.,

Adler, N. E., Morrow, J. D., & Cawthon, R. M. 2004). They have demonstrated that if you take everything personally, your telomeres will degrade. If you believe the negative thoughts in your head and the judgments from the past, your telomeres will degrade. In other words, stress will degrade your chromosomes.

Maybe things are not personal. Perhaps everything is not about you. In fact, what is *only* about you? Maybe it's just stress. Notice how your thinking may make it feel personal, how your thoughts may be on autopilot, and your reaction as well. When you change your thoughts and bring your attention to the present, you begin to respond differently. Begin to notice that you can be bigger than your thoughts. The "you" is more significant than your thoughts. The "you" can change your thoughts and notice your thoughts. You are not your thoughts.

When we are in the moment, we are using a different part of our brain. Being in the present allows activation in the left prefrontal cortex, regulating emotional balance. Studies have shown that the brain can change its structure to experience more happiness in eight weeks by using meditation. Yes, only eight weeks.

The hippocampus, the cerebellum, and the posterior cingulate cortex parts of the brain are involved in learning and meaning. The amygdala which is involved in emotions and motivation changes and calms the brain, reducing the flight, fight, and freeze response within. These brain parts can change with eight weeks of training in meditation. From the outside, meditation may look like a lot of nothing. Yet, we are changing our brain's activity as well as its structure.

Molecular biologists have found that we are able to up-regulate and down-regulate genes by being more present in our lives. Science shows when we are present and participate in our life, our brains change. As we work to grow a sense of presence, we grow regulation and propel ourselves forward. It opens a deep connection within ourselves, our culture, and our love, allowing us to regulate our bodies.

We are only alive when we are alive. When we think our lives are worthless, alone, having no self-esteem, we bring about our own sense of death: the death of the soul, the end of our truth, the death of self and our lives through thought. If we have died inside through negative thoughts, not allowing our truth to surface and grow, haven't we already died even before our body has died? This is what Jon Kabat-Zinn, founder of MBSR (mindfulness-based stress reduction) and internationally known for his work as a scientist, writer, and meditation teacher, argued in his thesis paper.

He explored how if we as individuals are not reaching for the truth of self—curious to see other perspectives, opening ourselves up to new experiences and kindness for ourselves and others—we are in a place of killing our own selves. We, by the thoughts we nurture, can be the death of us. Yet learning that there is the potential to live our lives by holding experiences in the present is powerful in many ways. It allows us to change our brain activity and brain structure. We do not need to start by thinking differently, but by noticing how we think, what we think about, and how the present differs from the past. Then, take in this mindful information rather than fill up an old box of the past. Walk away from disregarding what we are experiencing in the present. This present moment—without judgment and with understanding—is what allows our body to organize and reorganize our old automatic beliefs.

So, what is the point of mindfulness? The answer is simple: control, growth, happiness, and a deep sense of calm.

Are you in?

For more information on how to work on meditation or hear *Embrace* the meditation, go to www.HelloAnxiety.net.

CHAPTER TWENTY

BEES

Feathers Appear When Angles are Near
—Louise Soria a.k.a. LadyRed

Having already experienced Hurricane Florence, I made plans when I heard Hurricane Michael was heading toward us. The tall and scraggly grass waving at the neighbors had not been cut for a while, and with the amount of rainfall we were expecting, I decided it needed to be done now. And, yes, I do have boys in my home. They are ideal workers to wrangle lawn care and grass cutting for me at this point in their lives. Yet I also knew I needed to get in some exercise. Sitting all day talking with people is not ideal when it comes to physical strength. I had been working a lot, and the inactivity was beginning to eat at my body. So, I decided pushing the mower around was an excellent way to move and get in some cardio. Our front lawn is a hill and would allow me to dive into some good healthy movement.

The roar of the mower covered any other sounds as I plowed headlong into the brush and the pine straw. We have aggressive ivy actively attempting to take over the yard. The previous owner had planted two English ivy plants they had received as a present. Initially, in a planter, they decided to put them into the yard. BIG mistake. Now one-third of the lawn was covered with ivy that continues to grow even when sprayed or attacked with the mower—ivy growing up the trees, weathering pesticides, herbicides, and hatchet. It will not stop. Like Fear, it wants to take over. The neighbors hated it as it continued to migrate into their yard, and it was a battle we both took on together. First, the lawnmower would chop it down. We would then spray it and put down pine straw. It was a slow but steady battle.

So, there I was, cutting the grass, pushing the mower into the pine straw, and chopping away at the underbrush, when suddenly I felt this horrible sting on my leg! Not a yellow jacket nest! Painfully, this had happened before. I would be mowing and hit an underground yellow jacket nest. Threatened, they would become pissed off and start to swarm, attacking anyone within range.

Instinctively swatting the air around me, arms flailing, high stepping as though attempting to make some crazy dance moves, I let go of the mower and ran into the house. Once inside, upon inspection, my body seemed to have encountered only one sting, the one on my ankle. Running a credit card across my skin, I attempted to dislodge any stinger that may yet remain.

The pain was intense; burning sensations were shooting up my leg. But I knew it would subside with time. Deciding I might as well continue what I started, I gingerly looked outside for more yellow jackets. Thankfully there were none, so I finished the yard. But the pain did not finish; in fact, it increased and continued to expand. Pulsating with my heart, the discomfort grew louder as my leg complained to me. I have never experienced a sting that did not dissipate but continued to grow. Finally, the throbbing and intensity quieted down with a cold bag of ice draped across my ankle. Elevating my leg, I sat myself down on the couch.

Then the storm hit.

Dark clouds grew and consumed the blue sky. The air felt as though it was being sucked away, then suddenly released as it pummeled us with its intensity. Moving and whipping around, the house moaned, the air scattered the leaves, limbs broke, and a torrent of rain crashed down with the thunder. The lights went out. Darkness descended with the screaming storm outside. The entire power area in the city was knocked out. All of the stores, businesses, and homes lost power.

My leg was swelling, and the pain was growing as the storm escalated with each gust.

Twenty-four hours passed, and the driveway was cleared. Power had been restored to parts of the town as I ventured off to the office. My colleague stopped by to see how I was doing and how the building weathered the storm. I showed her my leg. It was still hurting, it was swollen, and red blotchy coloring was moving up the leg.

"What the hell are you doing at work? This is bad, very bad. You need a doctor."

She marked the redness with a sharpie and went out to see if anyone could see me. She walked around downtown knocking on doors to see if any doctor offices were open. There were none. Everyone was closed because of the storm. When she returned, she made me promise I would leave and go to an urgent care.

Her concern was a wake-up call. Here I am at work taking care of others yet not taking care of myself. What have I been justifying? I had been focused on my clients, but I know I must care for myself in order to continue to care for others. What type of example was I setting? How can I tell them to care for themselves when they are overwhelmed, juggling work, trauma, and family? What is my justification for setting this type of example?

I made some calls and found one urgent-care facility with power that was open. When I arrived, they listened to my story, looked at the leg, and told me they were pretty sure this was no yellow jacket sting.

"It appears to be a snakebite," the provider announced.

What?!

My husband had been traveling and came home to find me in pain, my leg swollen and red. I told him the doctor thinks a snake bit me. Georgia apparently has quite a few venomous snakes. He grabbed me, bundled me up, and hustled us off to Emory University Hospital.

Crowded with people, the chairs were overloaded as humanity gathered together huddled in the emergency room in need of help and assistance. Swathed in blankets, hunched over in pain, each of us waited to be seen. We waited for what seemed like forever in the emergency room. Finally, doors opened and names were called. With each opening of the door, heads swiveled to see if they would be next. Finally, we were in the back. Bustling nurses and technicians filled the halls as the curtains to our cubicle closed. Upon telling the doctor my story, the next thing I know I have thirteen doctors all around me. Emory is a teaching hospital, and everyone wanted in on the crazy woman who was bitten by a snake and was still walking around a few days later.

Snake enzymes interfere in normal blood coagulation through different mechanisms. Although significant progress has been made in understanding the structure, several questions are still being answered as more new anticoagulants are being discovered. Therefore, the doctors started checking my blood to see if they could isolate any of these enzymes and ensure the treatment met the situation's needs.

Apparently, the anticoagulant properties in the venom are the aspects that lead to death and cardiac arrest in people who encounter snakes. The doctors took blood, ran tests, and when the results came in, they find that, yes, I do have these enzymes in my system. A snake bit me.

It seems that, thankfully, I pulled away before both fangs were able to make a complete connection with my skin. Only one fang made contact, thus appearing only to be a yellow jacket sting. This fluke allowed my body to survive the onslaught of the venom. My blood was replenishing and working to establish coagulation. My heart was good. My blood was thin but all right. I needed to follow up with my doctor to monitor my continued progress. All of this is to say, even those who are aware often need others to say stop and point them toward self-care.

It was a crazy miracle.

CHAPTER TWENTY-ONE

ADDING NOT SUBTRACTING

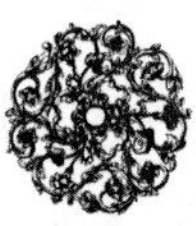

These pains you feel are messengers. Listen to them.

—Rumi

Each challenge we face provides a sense of direction. However, when you ask individuals if they would change their lives once they have perspective and have had time to look back and reflect, they typically say, "No, those challenges made me who I am today."

Each challenge I have encountered has allowed me to grow in clarity and understanding. Each one has offered me an opportunity to develop and honor self-care. Challenges are life-altering and value-enhancing. We begin to see how each trial helps to shape us. Each difficulty allows us to gain an understanding of ourselves and the world around us, providing an experience that would not have been there before. There is growth, purpose, meaning, anger, sadness, loss, joy, change. And if someone were to tell us about a certain experience, saving us from actually undertaking it ourselves, we most likely would not fully understand the learning we missed. More importantly, if someone told us, "Let me tell you what you could have learned," and stopped us from the experience, we would be denied the depth of understanding and learning that can only come from our own journey.

The beauty of connection is that each person in our lives is here to add to our experience and to add to our understanding of what we want and what we do not want. What we prefer and what we do not prefer. These people and experiences guide us. They lead us toward our best selves. They point us in the direction of cooperation rather than competition. Competition takes away; cooperation adds.

Another purpose of Anxiety is to help us recognize when we are subtracting from our lives. It guides us forward into life and situations. Its purpose is not to have us run from life but run into life. I tell my clients when they feel Anxiety, do not run from the situation—instead, run from the thought. Step into the situation and add to your life.

If you have misunderstood Anxiety, your life will become small and confined. You will find that you keep subtracting life from yourself. You will not go to the party, you will not go to the store, you will not drive, you will not explore people, you will not—not, not, not, subtraction, subtraction, subtraction. Eventually, your life is lost. You feel lost, lost in misery.

The person you were, the energy you had, is eaten away by Fear. Overwhelmed and filled with hurt, we often allow Fear to regulate and dismiss our own truth. The truth is you have come here to experience joy, to experience life. To try and to fail. To learn and to try again. To understand what you like, what you want, what feels best, and what you prefer. To step into something unfamiliar and make it your own. To change the world five seconds at a time and make it grow. To add, add, add—to yourself, your experiences, and others through understanding and cooperation.

When we step into our vulnerabilities, imperfections, and truth, we allow others to see who we are and learn how we became us and what has happened to define our needs. Understanding is formed. Even though others may not be able to feel our feelings, they can understand what we feel and possibly even why. When this occurs, connection, cooperation, healing, and compassion flow into us and into the collective world. Too much time is spent drawing our lines in the sand, stomping around pronouncing our rules and demanding everyone feels and thinks like us. Too often, we do not enhance ourselves by understanding why someone thinks or feels differently. We refuse to walk with them through their struggles and see their growth. We fall into competition, not cooperation.

Without addition, our lives may start out feeling comfortable and then move into stagnation. Tony Robbins says, "If you're not growing, you are dying." We need to add to ourselves, add to the world, to create and join with others.

Notice if you are subtracting from your life. Notice how often you pull back. Ask yourself, *What is going on with me, and where did this come from? Are feelings distracting me from my needs being met? Is there something that I like and would want more of in my life, and am I the one shutting it out? How am I choosing to move toward addition, and how am I allowing feelings to bring about subtraction?*

Build a relationship first with yourself. See what happens when you step back from judgment and competition. Notice and become aware. Be in your moment. Learn to respond to the moment, not to react to old information and experiences from the past. Work on deciding who you want to be no matter what the world throws at you. Notice what you need more of and how that need is addressed. Are you looking for consistency in a relationship so trust can grow? How are you showing yourself that you can trust yourself? How are you standing up for yourself? Are you being the trusted champion you deserve? Do you have your own back?

Do you want variety and new experiences? How are you adding these to your life? Are you putting yourself out there to meet new people and make new friends? When you were a child, how did you ask to play? How did you try on new people? As we age, we need to keep adding people into our lives. Our friends move, they change, they die, they grow. How are we doing the same? How are we moving, changing, and growing? Are you stagnating? Are you dying within?

Are your relationships challenging you to be your best person? Are you honoring that and resting when you need to process and be, cooperating within and with who you are? Do you listen to your body? Do you bully and yell at yourself? Have you become an abuser in your own life? Have you now become the person you said you would never be to yourself? Or do you send kindness and understanding inward? Compassion for what you have gone through and how you have survived?

How are you growing your life and giving to others? Whenever you add to someone else, you add to you. When we mentor, assist, lend a helping hand, we feel a sense of connection, the connection for which we are all looking. Remember this when you deny this feeling of connection to others when you shut others out, not allowing them the pleasure of helping or assisting you. You take away meaning and purpose if they have requested to lend you a hand, and you say, "No. I can do it myself." You are subtracting from your life and subtracting from the lives of those who care.

Remember: add to your life, do not subtract. Add, add, add.

CHAPTER TWENTY-TWO

WATER

We forget that the water cycle and the life cycle are one.
—Jacques Yves Cousteau

An elephant moves toward a watering hole, constant and precious. Warm and refreshing, the water calls many animals there, waiting, pressing, and reaching for what they know provides life. They have a need, and this need is required, it is not optional.

Our needs are the same. I interact with people who assume their needs often do not matter; their needs are placed into the background of life. They please everyone except themselves. They do for others and lose who they are and what they want. They discount themselves, swallow their voice, and judge their existence in a way that allows for no mercy. Shut off from the life cycle, they begin to wither and die. Like a plant or an elephant without water, their existence is limited, and without meeting their needs, the result is death—death of the soul, death of self.

All needs are a necessity, not an option. As we move through life's challenges, our needs may become prioritized differently, but they are required. When they are not met, we will find a way to have them in our life, whether by a healthy means or one that is unhealthy. The man who is ignored and has no internal reassurance will look elsewhere for this connection. The woman who is overwhelmed and lost her sense of self will reach for comfort and praise. The child who is alone and uncertain will bond with anyone who will accept them. Each of us will find our watering hole of life-giving needs.

There is an old proverb that speaks of the watering hole. The elephants regularly come to drink and be fulfilled. But slowly, the hole begins to dry, the rains have stopped, and the spot is unable to provide for the animals. Eventually, all that remains is dust and damp dirt. The animals continue to come looking for water, but the watering hole is unable to meet their needs. Still, they continue to come, over and over, till they are too weak to go on, stumbling till they fall onto the hard-packed earth. Yet other animals have seen the demise of the watering hole, and a decision was made. Rather than expecting the watering hole to support them, even when it cannot, they empower themselves and move on in search of a new source of water.

We have a choice and options when we direct ourselves. When we are in charge of our own needs and do not place that control externally, those needs can be met. When we love ourselves, we fill our internal basket with life-giving water. When we are proud of ourselves, we create a space within to receive from others. When we listen to what we prefer and reach for more, we empower our lives.

Just like when the water pipes suddenly break in our home, we begin to recognize how important water is to us. We notice how often we reach for the sink, wash our hands, flush the toilet, fill a pot. We are reminded of our need for water. When this need is denied, we miss it greatly. We pine for the ease, the supply that was always there. Difficulties ensue, and we do something. Calling for the pipes to be fixed. Suddenly, they are there, and water is flowing once again. We are so ecstatic and relish in the availability of water. We rejoice and celebrate the wonder that our need is thankfully being met, enjoying the ease of reaching for refreshment. Then slowly and eventually, it moves to the background, ever-present but no longer in the forefront of our mind.

Like all needs, when we have an easy supply, we often do not notice what is there for us. Yet if it dries up or is removed, we experience turmoil and loss. Those things we do not have, we prioritize more. Those we do have; we may fail to acknowledge. Gratitude helps us to notice these constants; the ones that fall into the background of our lives. Challenges bring forward awareness of the water that has been turned off. Yet all of our needs are important—the ever-present ones and the ones we may not be receiving. And just like we cannot exist without water, we cannot live without our needs being met. Without them, we will wither and die inside.

Remember needs are a necessity, not an option. When they are turned off, we can reach for our power within to supply them for ourselves. We can ask for the cookie, make the cookie, send love inside, be grateful for the small stuff, or call for the plumber. We can show kindness and understanding to ourselves rather than hold a court of severe judgment. We can stop terrorizing ourselves. We can water our own neural network and move toward what we know we prefer, want, and need.

Remember, you deserve to have water. Do something about it or go find it for yourself and enjoy it.

MIRACLE SEVEN

CHAPTER TWENTY-THREE

THE "C" WORD

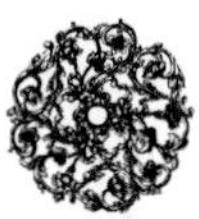

Cancer opens many doors. One of the most important is your heart.

—Greg Anderson

"Yes, you definitely have breast cancer. It is triple positive and very aggressive. We need to start addressing it now."

A few months before, I was showering and noticed a lump in my breast. Dang lumps! I would get these all the time. They were dense tissue typically caused by hormonal changes in my cycle. I started my regimen of warm compresses and ibuprofen. I even called the imaging center and asked if I could schedule an appointment without a doctor's visit. I get these lumps so frequently, and it just seemed like an unnecessary step in the process to spend extra time going to the doctor's office. One additional visit that I knew would slow things down.

"No, you need to have a doctor order the imaging."

Damn.

As I suspected, the doctor could not get me in for a week. I kept using ibuprofen and warm clothes. Finally, my doctor affirmed at my visit it was likely a fibroid, as I was prone to them, but it would be best to get it checked out. A week later, the obligatory breast-smashing, trauma-inducing scan was followed by a gentle ultrasound. My breasts are small and dense, so they smash and bruise me up every time I have a mammogram. They always end up having to do an ultrasound so they can actually see something. But do they start with the ultrasound? The gentle warm gel and easy procedure? No.

I swear if men had to have their private parts smashed between two cold plates till their eyes watered, they would figure out a different way. Oh, wait a minute! They have. Men get a blood test.

This was not a fibroid.

Excuse me? Did you say this is not a fibroid? It's always a fibroid. You must have someone else's chart. Can you please recheck you have the chart for Natalie Kohlhaas, as this is not my story?

"We are not sure what it is, so we will have to reschedule you to come back and do a biopsy of the area."

Of course, this will take another week. Now I am three weeks out from finding the lump. My husband happened to be out of town during this visit. He was returning in a few weeks, so I decided it was best to keep this to myself until I knew for certain there was indeed anything to be concerned over. Deciding not to go through this alone, I called my best friend in the area and asked her if she would go with me. We made a nice day of it, eating lunch at a new restaurant across the street from the hospital. Unfortunately, she had to wait in the waiting room while they performed the horrendous biopsy on me. I was so black and blue that even my oncologist was concerned with the bruising a few weeks later. I don't know what the heck the doctor was thinking, but it definitely had nothing to do with making me comfortable or calm.

They came in and decided which tracing unit they would install into the breast. This is apparently the way they track where they have done a biopsy, and it also helps the doctor find the area they may need to remove later on in the process. The tracer is a small piece of metal they place inside. They referred to it as my internal tattoo. Once the doctor decided what would be placed inside of me, he gave me some lidocaine to numb the area. I let him know that I take quite a bit of time to numb over, and he would need to wait for a moment.

He told me, "Nonsense, everyone numbs over at the same rate."

"Well, I do not numb quickly. I want some extra time before you go in."

He grabbed a needle and said, "I'll just give you some extra lidocaine."

As he is dug into my breast, I was in so much pain my breath caught as my body tensed and froze. Afterward, I sat in a small cold hallway waiting to hear some information, holding my breast, waiting and hoping for the lidocaine to kick in eventually. Twenty minutes later, they informed me we had to smash my breast again to make sure they got the tracer in the right place.

"You have to be kidding me. What about the warm gel and a soothing sweeping ultrasound?"

Ha! No.

Once the last, horrible, painful smashing was complete, I was put once again into the cold hallway. Here I waited. And waited.

Finally, someone came out and told me, "We got the sample. Go home, and your doctor will call you."

My husband arrived home to plans we made to attend his favorite music venue in downtown Atlanta. It's always a great time. Friends, food, drink, and of course, music filled the days and nights. Wanting to enjoy the weekend, I held off telling him about my ordeal. I was even able to hide my swollen and bruised breast. But once the weekend was done, I sat him down and shared what was happening. Of course, we were both thinking this will be fine. This isn't my story.

It was 9:20 p.m. when the phone rang.

My husband answered. "It's your doctor."

Just know that when your doctor calls you late in the evening, it's typically not great news.

"Natalie, your results are in. You have cancer. It is triple positive, and I want you to meet with an oncologist as soon as possible."

The table was sturdy and the chair steady as my primary care provider went through a lot of information that I was writing down. I had no idea what the hell she was talking about. It was a whole new world of vocabulary, an entirely new world of doctors, of being out of control and pushed around. What I did know was I had to reach for myself, my values, my truth, listen to my superpower or I would become redefined by an illness.

Thank goodness I found the lump early.

It was a miracle.

CHAPTER TWENTY-FOUR

TRUTH HIGHLIGHTS OUR PATH

Trusting yourself means living out what you already know to be true.

—Cheryl Strayed

So, our friend Anxiety is here trying to help us find our truth. How the heck do we do this? To find your truth, you must first look at your values. Our values may rearrange themselves over time, but they do stay the same in fundamental ways of self and understanding.

In looking at our topic on the table, we find our old beliefs about ourselves and how the world works. Once we begin to challenge these imposed self-problems and start dismantling these old beliefs that no longer serve us as we work through therapy, we now need to see what we believe and who we are today. Who are we? What do we understand about ourselves, and how do we see ourselves as we move forward?

It is always interesting to work on values with a client. All of us have clear values when it comes to our kids or our coworkers in how they need to be treated, seen, heard, and loved. Yet once we talk about ourselves, it's often very different. This is where we diverge and get off track.

I use a sheet of fundamental values so clients can see where they are currently, what is important to them at this stage of life, and how they are succeeding at their values. Each of these values is then translated into action.

Value Examples

> *Parenting: Parenting is important to me. I want to be involved in my children's lives and be a good role model.*
> *Friendship: Is a building block for my life. I learn to be there in times of need as I give and receive support with laughter and acceptance.*

Asking yourself a few fundamental questions about yourself and your direction can move you toward opening up to an understanding of what you know and what you need to become clear on. Why is this important to you? How are you succeeding at this?

On a scale of one to five, rate your level of truth on these statements:

- I am clear on my values, strengths, and weaknesses.
- I know what I want.
- I am clear about my goals and passions.
- I know how to get what I want.
- I have a plan to achieve my dreams.

As we work on defining values, I often see a pattern emerge:

"I see myself as a helper; leadership is important to me; respect is a core value I know I want to achieve; family is my main focus."

Whatever that primary value is, this is what I build off. This becomes the stepping-stone for their new story and their truth at this time in their life.

I have each of my clients begin to work on Dr. Galen E. Cole's Life Script Restructuring method of understanding their goals. We break it down into DO, HAVE, FEEL, and BE goals:

- In life, how do you want to FEEL?
- Who is the person you want to BE?
- What is it you see yourselves DOING?
- What do you want to HAVE in your life?
- How do I love myself?

All of these aspects need to align with one's values. Without this alignment, you will push yourself into territory that is unethical or off-kilter. Your internal values are the guardrails for your life. Without them, you can experience Anxiety, shame, and depression.

All of us need these guardrails. We need some type of security to help us align with our true selves. We identify these feelings as negative emotions, yet a miraculous maker put this emotional guidance system into place. It assists us and allows us to see when we are no longer heading down a path of light, love, and truth.

With each client, together we work on the clarity of their future self. Not the one that the past wrote for them. Wayne Dyer often talked about a boat moving along the water of life. The boat creates a wake behind it. But it is not the wake that keeps the boat moving. It is the energy of the present moment that powers and energizes the boat. The wake does not direct the boat. The driver decides on their pathway and direction to move. The wake is there and has happened, but it does not power or direct the boat of your life. Knowing where you came from is important, but allowing it to dissipate like a wake in the water opens us up toward a path of love and understanding: We can create in this direction. We can reach for good. We can experience peace and ease. We are the drivers of our lives.

Ask yourself about your future self:

Who is my future self?
What is my social world like?
What service do I provide?
What skills do I have?

We begin to work on becoming intentional about what we want. The direction we are going and heading. We begin to step into our lives, feeling the emotions that are there in front of us, stepping into the feelings as though they have already happened.

I tell my clients they need to know where they are aiming. If you throw random darts, someone will get hurt. Let's define you, and your space, and your wants first. Let's define the person that became lost in the cycle of Fear and repression.

Let's find you.

For more information on values and how your values are aligned with your truth, go to www.HelloAnxiety.net.

CHAPTER TWENTY-FIVE

LOSS OF CONTROL

Loss of control is always the source of fear. It is also, however, always the source of change.

—James Frey

I was in the process of signing a lease for a new three-thousand-square-foot building when we got the "C" word. In two weeks, it would have been ours. It was finally coming together, with nine offices and a large training room awaiting people and a renewed purpose. I would have set up my own center, my own institute with like-minded practitioners, and a training facility. It was something I had been working toward for quite a while. Finally, it seemed like it was going to happen.

I had gathered an acupuncturist, two massage therapists, a reiki healer, two psychotherapists, and a nutritional therapist. The building was perfect—large and expansive, soft carpet underfoot, and it had a built-in sound system. There were windows allowing light to stream in, illuminating the space that opened to offices and restrooms.

Then comes the loss of control, loss of decisions, loss of vision of who I am . . . Friggin' cancer?! I was so pissed!

There is nothing more difficult for someone who struggles with Anxiety than feeling a loss of control. Control is everything; control over your own body is imperative. Without this control, the struggle takes over.

Suddenly, everyone was telling me what to do, when to do it, and how to do it—everything that goes entirely against my sense of free will and sense of self. I had to put a stop to it! I sat down with a trusted girlfriend and went through the business piece with her. She wisely told me to back off and let go of the business. I did have an opportunity to move forward with another team member's help, but she decided to move forward without me. It was decided: I needed to walk away and focus once again on myself.

I had decided on how I wanted to address cancer, but no one would give me the space to move in this direction. Instead, I felt like the answer I kept receiving was, "No, you're not allowed, no control, no decisions."

This is where I rebelled. I began to interview my doctors. I needed to have some control and some ability to make my own decisions.

I remember being asked, if it were up to me, would I go through chemotherapy? The honest answer: *Hmmm . . . maybe not*. But I had a family and a husband, and if I chose not to go through chemotherapy, they would have been so stressed, worried, and devastated with my decision. I would never have been able to focus on myself. So, I had to figure out how to put my methods and the doctors' methods together.

This is where my conversation with my girlfriend began, on how to meld these two worlds. I explained that I refused to fight with myself. This seemed so crazy to me. If I was fighting with myself, that meant I would have to lose. I would win, and I would lose. This makes no sense to me. As a therapist, we know fighting does not bring about results. It only shuts out others and causes division. I needed to bring about connection and fusion.

As I discussed my concerns with my girlfriend, I explained that I saw it as a need to resolve an issue.

Resolve was and would be my word, not *fight*. I envisioned everyone sitting at a table, two sides with opposing views. What did they both need? What was wanted? What could I give to appease their concern? Like two warring sides, they needed a mediator. My girlfriend told me to view the chemotherapy as the mediator, the aspect that would allow both sides to come to the table. This would bring me and cancer together to express what was needed, what was wanted, and what would help. Now this was something I could wrap my head around!

As I interviewed my future doctors, I let them know I would be meditating, using acupuncture, reiki, and hypnotherapy. They needed to be on board and supportive of me and these therapies. The doctors I chose agreed. I asked if they would give me six weeks. I would have the lump gone within six weeks. Sadly, they said NO—too aggressive, too much risk.

I prescribe to and have listened to the teachings of Dr. Joe Dispenza for many years. Dr. Dispenza is a doctor of chiropractic with postgraduate training in the fields of neuroscience and neuroplasticity, quantitative electroencephalogram (QEEG) measurements, and epigenetics. He purports that we are in control of our own body's blueprint. When we go through life based on the past, we are conditioning ourselves for the past, past fears, and the "what if" self-induced problems. We spoke the same language, and I had enough on my plate. I certainly was not going to add any more problems—no thought distortions, self-induced problems, and no fights with myself.

It was once again time for me to focus on me. It was time for me to put all of my training into place and revisit my sense of knowing. Do the work. I had to find my creativity and ability to grow through this process—time to remind myself of what I had learned and what I did know. I was not wrong. I had gone through life's challenges and knew what worked for me. My perception of life, my insight, they were here with me. It was time for me to assure myself and my family that I was listening, staying on course, and not dropping into panic filled with assumptions—reaching for my truth, my love, and my capabilities.

No Fear, no war, only love and resolve.

CHAPTER TWENTY-SIX

CREATIVITY

People never learn by being told, they have to find out for themselves.

—Paulo Coelho

Creativity is only now being seen as an essential part of growth and self in mental health. Through neuroplasticity and the science of the brain, we have learned that brains grow when we are actively feeding and updating our perceptions. We are creating new pathways and rewiring our present. We are gaining control of our emotions while in the present moment. When we are in play and creative, we open up to the present and our intuition.

According to Brené Brown, unused creativity is dangerous. She explores ten guideposts to wholehearted living in her book, *Daring Greatly: How the Courage to be Vulnerable Transforms the Way We Live, Love, Parent, and Lead.* She explains that we need to recognize ourselves as creative beings and find time to enjoy creation in our moments of play. Author and researcher Stewart Brown calls play "time spent without purpose." The action we are doing needs to be bigger than the purpose. Time spent with no expectation, no judgment, no perfection, no plan, no pressure, just being fully in the moment and following your joy and intuition—for me, this is play.

The opposite of play is depression. Studies have shown that when we engage in creativity or play, we grow and shape our brains. We open new neural pathways and allow for creation. It is deeper than gender, more resonant than fun, and produces new thoughts. Play helps us override an old brain survival nature (competition) and opens up to cooperation. We can think about it as a way to build connection, collaboration, and experimentation. Social play allows us to feel a part of something, not alone, and it provides an opportunity for emotional regulation. Imaginative and narrative play helps us with the stories we tell ourselves and others. Whether imaginative, social, or narrative, all play is born from curiosity and exploration.

Remember that curiosity and a willingness to explore are some of the main fighters of Fear. Exploration and curiosity fight predisposed automatic thoughts and feelings. It closes down judgment and opens us up to gathering information. When we have knowledge, we can then decide what to do and how we feel about the information: *What do I want to do with this information? What about this information is accurate, and how much more information do I need to make a decision? What type of response would allow me to be the person that feels my best?*

Creativity propels curiosity and engages us in a place of play within our brains. Remember, when the brain gets the survival switch engaged, information in the present is often overridden by the past. Yet when we move into play and kindness, we open ourselves up to curiosity and connection, creating a healthier response.

Sitting in curiosity allows us to explore intuition. Intuition is a way to listen to our own healthier responses and is different than feeling and thinking. It is an inner knowing that goes beyond your thinking. Believe it or not, our hearts are now known to have their own brains. The heart has something known as the "little brain," and science has shown that the heart thinks. It makes decisions without the "big brain." This heart is home to some forty thousand sensory neurites. These neurites make up the little brain within our hearts.

The Heart Math Institute (HMI), founded in 1991, has been a forerunner of research on decreasing stress and working toward heart and mind alignment. HMI has found that the heart can receive information before our conscious brain does. In fact, over thirteen thousand biochemical reactions occur when we align the little brain of our heart with our minds. It turns on our immune response, our anti-aging hormones, cardiovascular health, and information into an understanding of what we recognize, as a knowing of what we need.

Intuition utilizes this little brain. It is emotionally neutral, which is funny when you think it resides in our hearts. The little brain helps us to recognize our direction and needs. Intuition is what comes out of your heart before there is any hesitation. Intuition, like Anxiety, will not talk you in or out of something with words in your head. It will start out as a nonverbal action. If you have a knowing without words, your intuition is activated. With intuition you do not have an explanation. There is no past information to push you forward. Recognizing your intuition is opening up to curiosity and exploration. This is brain-heart intuition.

INTUITION

> *If you know you want to get a job, listen to your heart. It tells you this is in your best interest. You listen to this intuition and step into the phone call before you talk yourself out of it. You know you want the job, so you're just going to call and see what happens. You have no explanation as to why you want to call that particular place, except it feels right.*

When we become curious and explore and approach the world as our own place of play, we can start to step into a creative space without judgment. Filled with cooperation and kindness, open to sharing our imperfections and asking for our needs, this space is one without pressure or expectation.

Here, we begin to find ourselves and our truth.

CHAPTER TWENTY-SEVEN

ILLUSION

Love yourself like your life depends on it, because it does.
—Anita Moorjani

I know control is an illusion. But when we suddenly have the illusion thrown in our face, it's a shock. It's then that we need to decide how to regain ourselves and learn how to respond rather than react. How do we protect and love ourselves and those who are important to us? We work on regrouping and opening up to all that we need and all that we know.

Cross-legged, I feel the warmth of my husband's hand, reassuring, and firm. It's our twenty-fifth wedding anniversary, yet our mood is not celebratory. As I sit with the uncomfortable exam table underneath me, the air is hanging heavy, dripping off the bland white walls, puddling onto the cold, sterile floor as we stare at the paper with the diagrams the doctor is discussing. Hunched over, pointing to the paper with deft fingers, the oncologist explained the treatment options in front of us.

"You have three options," she explained.

Three different chemical choices with different durations, processes, and direction. And also, the surgical options. Yet nothing feels like an option. Each doctor we meet with goes through the same things, the same horrendous procedures, the same standard—no option.

I hunker down and dig in. *What happens with these procedures? How will they affect me? What does all of this mean, and how will this affect my body? Why are these the options in front of us? Where is the information based and coming from concerning these options? What and why? And anyway, I thought you worked from the oath* do no harm?

I tell the doctor, "So, my understanding is you are going to pump my body full of poison and hope the cancer dies before I do?"

"Ah, well the harm you will encounter will be less than the harm which will come your way if you do not follow one of these options."

Really, this is the approach?

"You will experience fatigue, diarrhea, nausea, cramping, loss of taste, sores in the mouth, body aches and pain, brain fog, and constipation. Your intestinal tract will be attacked, as well as all the cells that quickly divide."

I ask about hair loss.

"Well, yes, you will lose your hair."

"Is it a definite that I will lose my hair?"

Now with all the things they had told me, you would think this would not be the biggest or the worst part of the horrible story. But for me, the hair loss was the hardest to process. For me, it represented the loss of control—a subtraction to my life.

I had decided no subtraction, only adding to my life. As crazy as it sounds, of all the things, the phrase "you have cancer" was not the most difficult to allow. It was being told I would lose my hair! What the heck? This was the part that filled my body with sadness?

Sobs filled my heart and began to wander slowly down my face as the situation started to sink in. Why was this so hard? It's just hair. Why was I so upset about the hair, for goodness' sake? Slowly, it began to make sense—the realization growing inside.

I would not have control. I would not have the ability to

decide with whom I wanted to share my struggles. Who could enter into my life in ways that were personal and raw. All of that was going to be gone for me. Everyone would know my medical condition and see it all over my body. I felt as though I was losing one more piece of control. The control that is so important to us Anxiety people.

I began by reaching out to my closest group, having conversations with those I loved, and those important to me. It started with our children. Having to sit down and let them know what was in front of us, talking about percentages and treatment plans and how I would need their time and presence during the process.

I leaned into my support and let go of the illusion of control.

CHAPTER TWENTY-EIGHT

DECLUTTERING THE BRAIN

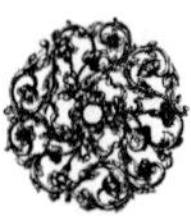

We must substitute faith for fear, for fear is only inverted faith; it is faith in evil instead of good.

—Florence Scovel Shinn

Remember, Anxiety is your best friend. It will never, ever give up on you. Anxiety may at first appear to be negative but remember it's the gatekeeper for Fear. Anxiety monitors Fear and continually keeps it in check. It assesses when Fear is out of control, and when it is, it will get your attention so you can shift back into life.

But what about shame and depression? If we continue to disregard our friend Anxiety and push it to the side, knocking it down, eventually, we become numb—numb to our thoughts, numb to our best friend, numb to the world. We often experience this numbness as depression. Often people who experience depression state they don't feel anything—a never-ending numbness with sadness holding them hostage. Now your friend Anxiety still will not give up. Late at night, Anxiety is there as you are trying to fall asleep, and rather than listen to it, notice if you become incredibly annoyed.

When we are beginning to fall asleep, our brains move from consciousness to unconsciousness. If you have become numb to your emotional guidance system, then Anxiety must find a way to reach you. It may work with you even while you are sleeping. As it works to rid you of all of those horrid thoughts, you may experience bad dreams or nightmares. This is how Anxiety allows you to get rid of the ideas—by emptying your brain during rest with the hope that you will awaken refreshed and clear.

But if you have pushed away too many emotions and focused on too many negative thoughts, Anxiety may have more trash to go through than time allows. Here's how I explain it to my clients:

Your Mind's Building

> Your mind is a large, looming, office building. Inside are your search engine employees, all of whom have access to the information about your life. As expected, there is a big room with "the table." Here, they have been working all day, drinking coffee, making copies, sending memos, and making a right mess. Now at night, the cleaning crew comes in. Their supervisor is Anxiety. Anxiety has them go through all the nonsense and clean it all out. Anxiety wants the cleaning crew to get the building pristine and clutter-free, with no sign of the wackiness that was being thrown at you yesterday. So, Anxiety sends in the cleaners.
>
> As they go through all the rubbish, you experience dreams. Dreams are filled with all of the overused, unnecessary emotions of the day. The dreams may not make visual sense, but emotionally they make perfect sense. We feel those emotions as they release them out of the building and into the dumpster.
>
> Now, if the cleaning crew has eight hours to get everything all cleared out and you sleep for eight

> hours, then great. You will wake up and feel better, those problems have melted away, and now you can clearly see what you need or want to do. But if you wake up in the middle of the night, let's say 3:30 a.m., and then you sit and ponder all of the rubbish, so you can't fall asleep till 5:30 a.m., and then you have to get up at 6:30 a.m. . . . well, they didn't get enough time to clear out the trash.
>
> Now, the search monster employees start promptly at 6:30 a.m., as soon as you wake and, of course, they continue their process of making more trash. Once again, the next night, the cleaning crew comes in and now they have the leftover trash from the day before plus the new day's rubbish to get rid of in eight hours! So how do you help them out? Once again, you wake up and only give them six hours to get the job done. Ugh! You can see where this is going.

This process of cleaning out the brain is known as venting. While we sleep, our brain washes away the trash of the day and vents out all the unnecessary stuff we may be holding onto. Yet no matter how much is removed or not removed, we hold onto our values. So, when you cannot sleep, you end up with more and more trash that is not taken out. This builds up the rubbish and increases the likelihood of depression and feelings of Anxiety.

This may also be why people who experience depression want to sleep so much. They know they need time to take out the trash. Unfortunately, it can also lead to more bad information and feelings of shame: *You need to get up. You're so lazy. All you do is lie around.* It becomes a balancing game—sleeping and engaging, doing, and resting. A game that most are not prepared to play alone. The brain needs to reset, and sleep helps with this process. Also, watching how much trash we continue to add each day also is extremely important. We can add less and allow the cleaners to make their way through the garbage quicker. We can work with our friend rather than against them. We can be part of the solution and connect with our sense of self, creativity, and compassion.

Reaching for who we are, our values, and our truth allows us to experience a sense of knowing—not feeling, but knowing truth, logic, and self. This is what each of us is continually reaching for and understanding deep within that we deserve.

If you can't sleep, please be mindful and attempt to fill your trash during the day with splendor, gratitude. and laughter. Step into creativity and experience a safe and beautiful place within your own mind's building.

CHAPTER TWENTY-NINE

HELLO, HOW ARE YOU DOING?

The way attention is focused changes and helps balance the brain.

—Dr. Dan Siegel

Who did I want to be? What would I feel? What would I have? Health is where I was going to put my focus as I redefined control for myself. Using all the techniques and training I had at hand, I was ready to move forward. Once I decided to address my illness in my own way, I reached out to my family and friends and asked for their support. I knew I could not do this alone, and I needed to have my support team. Without them, I would be lost.

EMAIL SENT TO FRIENDS AND FAMILY:

Hello, how are you doing?
Normally I answer, "Great . . . how are you?" but nowadays, I am placed in a different situation, and for all of you whom I love and consider my close friends, I am sharing with each of you the new challenge that lies ahead.

For those I have had the opportunity to talk with, you have heard that I recently found a lump in my right breast. After multiple doctor visits and discussions, we now know that this lump will not easily disappear. And so, it seems as though I am about to begin a new journey. Thankfully, this journey has amazing odds in my favor. I'm healthy; hell, the doctors even say I'm young—ha! But also, I am blessed to have found this very early on. So, as I'm not able to call and discuss this with each person as I wish I could, due to time, emotional energy, and the demands of life, Curtis suggested this email to share the news with everyone.

So here it is . . .

Due to the findings in my biopsy, the doctors want us to move quickly. Apparently, this lump is dividing fast and is aggressive. Because of this, the doctors have done much research on this type, and they have targeted therapies to assist in the reduction of its growth. This is great news. Yet, due to its aggressive nature, they also are requiring an extensive treatment plan. So, I will be doing chemotherapy for five months, a lumpectomy if all goes well, daily radiation for three to five weeks, pill chemotherapy for one year, and hormone therapy for the next five years. This has a great success rate, and the plan is to be dancing and laughing with everyone by 2020.

Well, as amazing and wonderful as all of those options sound, it doesn't quite fill me completely with joy and wonder. So, while the doctors have their plan, I also am formulating my own. Many of you know that my mindset is of a holistic, positive nature. So, to maintain my views and sense of self, I am embarking on a collaborative process where I can meld my views and beliefs with the doctors' methods. This is where I am going to ask for your assistance. If you are willing to be a part of my positive movement through this, I welcome all of your help. First, it will be important for me to maintain a sense of self and not be seen as an illness. Second, I know that holding a positive perspective and a sense of love will sustain me.

So here is my concept of empowerment and treatment:

I believe that I am part of something larger than myself, and that "something" is a connective force that joins each of us on this planet. I view this force as a positive and loving energy that moves through every atom and molecule around us and in us. I also believe each of us has the free will to reach for our own thoughts and feelings, which in turn creates our emotions. No one can choose my thoughts or decide what and how I am allowed to feel. And when I am feeling happy and joyous, that feeling is contagious in the same way when someone is pissed and angry—everyone is able to pick up on the tension and vibrations being emitted. I also feel it is the positive and loving emotions that sustain us.

*Being a brain geek and neuroscience nerd, I understand the power of our thoughts, vibration, and metaphysical possibilities. So, I ask that each of you think of me in the future and present as happy, smiling, and experiencing love. Your faith and positive thoughts will help guide me and provide me with strength. I also am coining a new phrase for myself. I am "*resolving*" my issue. I do not like the idea of* fighting *with my body. Fighting does not make for a happy relationship or a happy Natalie. So rather than fighting with myself, I will be resolving the issues that need to be addressed and attempting to meet the needs of my own cells and body. I am working with a nutritional coach, acupuncturist, reiki healer, and massage therapist, in addition to my oncologists. I am doing daily meditations/prayers and engaging in a diet of uplifting videos and shows. I have no doubt that I will be fine and dandy soon enough, and with your help, love, and positive thoughts, we, as a family, with our amazing friends by our side, will get through this gracefully.*

I hope we can add you to our team, and you will allow us to reach and sustain ourselves with your hope, love, and understanding.

Please use this email to reach me if you have thoughts,

questions, or just want to share. We will not be posting on social media about this journey but will be using this email address to communicate with those who wish to share news and positive, loving energy.

Thank you, my beautiful friends and family.

Much love, I hope you are doing great!

Natalie

This is how I chose to start my journey. I also refused to say the word "cancer." Instead, I said "lump," "bump," "concern"—anything except "cancer." I did not want to give it any power. And the C-word is so filled with emotion.

Knowing how powerful words and emotions can be, I did not want anything except the best and clearest feeling in my life. I was choosing what and how I was going to feel. I was moving forward, and that was toward a bright and wonderful future. I am blessed with fantastic support, and this support allowed me to find the right team. Without my husband's work connections, who immediately got on the phone and set up appointments for me, we would have been struggling. My team was and is amazing! They were willing to work with me as I worked on myself. I made my own decisions as much as possible. I told them I could have the lump gone in six weeks. Everyone scoffed and patted me on the head as I stepped into my cave, a safe and beautiful place in my own mind.

So, my newest journey had begun. Hello Anxiety, my old friend, here you are once again by my side.

CHAPTER THIRTY

PERSONAL VISION

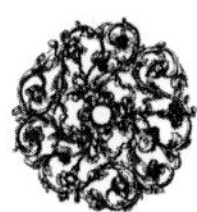

Your personal vision will become clear only when you can look into your heart.
Who looks outside, dreams; who looks inside, awakes.

—Carl Jung

Having a vision is not the same as setting goals. Goals push you toward accomplishing tasks, while a vision pulls you toward your passion, like a magnet. It's necessary to have goals, no doubt. But you must also have a greater vision. Your goals will help you reach your vision.

Having a vision of your future "you" will give you a sense of purpose. It will give you glimpses of what is possible, creating a desire to grow and improve. It will also help you push forward through the obstacles and hardships that emerge on your path.

Each client I work with eventually gets to a place of vision. This is where the combination of values and desires move together. We work on defining their desires, their feelings, their wants, their being. Then, they move into seeing and hearing their emotions. This is where I once again use Dr. Galen's method of Life Script Restructuring and M-CBT. Each person creates their own emotional connection utilizing an image combined with sound. It may be a picture they have drawn. It may be one that they have found. It may be one that they have looked for. But each one means something to them. Each one elicits emotion and a feeling. Functional Imagery Training helps clients to connect to the person they know they are aiming for. Studies have shown that imagery can be used to help control competitive Anxiety levels and enhance self-confidence. More and more is being found to support the use of imagery through brainspotting, hypnotherapy, and /or imagery combined with statements of purpose.

When a person wants to share their feelings or what is important to them, they often will show a picture. For example, rather than telling you they have a small dog that is brown with a white stomach, they know an image will elicit more feelings than the information about the size and color of the animal. When they show us a picture, a warmth flows over us as we look at the soft puppy with big, clear, open eyes. While the information may be useful, it is not connected in the same way as images are to our emotions.

Tone and inflection are important ways we intake emotional meaning and purpose. We can hear the meaning and emotion with the use of words. Movies are the king of emotional pull. They use pictures, words, and music to create a mood and emotionally draw you in.

When we see and hear information, it creates a larger bond to our emotional bank. Just as when we hear a song, it might transport us back to a time when we first heard the song, or it may fill us with strong emotion. Music is a powerful vibration. It can motivate us. It can calm us. It can excite us. It is filled with intensity.

Like our own movie, we can create a bank of pictures, words, and music to elicit the desired emotions we hold for our future self. When we have our picture, our song, and a statement that resonates with us, we have a powerful vision that helps us stay focused. It connects on many levels. It can remind us of who we are, who we want to be, or why we are working on this goal. Even when it is difficult, our goal is emotionally there.

Example: I wish to be independent.

- Why do you want to achieve this particular goal?
- What good things may happen if you reach this goal?
- What bad things may happen if you achieve this goal?
- What bad things may happen if you don't reach this goal?
- How will things be different if you achieve this goal?

Rehearsal allows the brain to emotionally experience things that have not happened as though they have. Our brain fires precisely as though the experience has happened when we rehearse it and feel it and "experience it." This is creation. We are creating new neural networks. Neuroplasticity has shown us, through FMRI's, that our brains are firing as though what we are thinking and feeling is actually happening. Just like when we rehearse something bad, our brains truly believe it is happening in real-time, almost like a flashback.

The same happens with good thoughts: we can create new neural networks in our brains. These networks allow us to send positive messages that haven't happened to our brain as though they have already happened. This is how we can create. We create new pathways, new parts of our brain, new feelings, new experiences. This is the science of manifestation. When they say we can create our future, they mean we can feel our future, experience our future, and our brain thinks it is true and happening and then grows into that realm.

This is where hypnotherapy is so very powerful. Clinical hypnotherapy allows us to experience the world in a way where we can choose. We can look at the past and then decide how we would rather have moved through that time, what we would have said if we could have, what we would have done if we had the power and had been safe. While in hypnosis, we are safe, and we are in control. We can freeze time, speed up time, notice what we didn't have time to notice. We can use this information as we see ourselves in the future. We can move and fly forward and become the person we always wanted to be. And while we do so, we are feeling it, we are experiencing it, we are living it.

Once we have established new neural networks and rehearsed these new feelings, we can feed these networks. I explain to my clients these networks look like plants growing into trees. When we look at them in FMRI's, we can see them growing. As they are growing, we get to decide which pathway we want to feed: the negative or the positive. Caroline Leaf, a cognitive neuroscientist specializing in cognitive and metacognitive neuropsychology, has shown that the mind can change the brain. We know that there is neuroplasticity. We know that the more time we spend rehearsing the positive, the more those positive plants are watered. The more we spend time rehearsing and feeling negative thoughts, the more we water the negative plants.

As the old story goes, the young Native American told his grandfather, "I often feel as though there is a good wolf and a bad wolf inside of me. They are constantly fighting. I do not know which one will win."

The grandfather turned to him. "My son, this is easy: whichever one you feed."

We are always working on which neural pathway we are feeding. We are our own brain creators, and we get to decide which plant we want to water or neural network we wish to feed.

For assistance on creating a personal vision, choose a www.HelloAnxiety.net membership and step into your good wolf.

<u>CHAPTER THIRTY-ONE</u>

CHEMOTHERAPY

Every problem is a gift—without problems we would not grow.

—Tony Robbins

The horror can be withstood. I approached "treatment" as a way to have time, focus, meditate, help me on my journey, and as a means to water my good, positive plant and feed my good wolf. I looked at each treatment as a gift of downtime, an opportunity to reach out in prayer, spend time with my family, and connect with myself. I knew a part of me was still above me and watching over me. I was there looking down. My family members and friends were here with me supporting me, hoping I would accept this challenge as I agreed to approach myself and my world with a sense of openness.

I tried my best. But chemotherapy is horrible and sucked. My strength waned, my head spun, my body rebelled—I broke out all over, my lymphatic system filled and swelled. My mouth lost taste, and pain filled the place that offered comfort with displeasure. My stomach tried to expel the toxins; my bowels churned and expressed their irritation. With each treatment, the intensity of revolt increased.

I fought back with love and acceptance, with a knowing that I would resolve any discord in my body. I comforted the feelings and acknowledged the hurt, working to be with myself and honor the difficulties.

I recognized the chemicals would not hurt me unless I gave into the idea of doubt. My faith needed strengthening. My soul needed to be fed. My breath was slow and, at times, difficult but a steady reminder of my gift. My gift was to choose how I wished to feel today, who I wanted to reach for and hold, how my messages would be expressed, and where my focus and time were spent.

I spent my time often listening to my family's laughter from afar and relishing in its expressive nature, noticing how vegetables were still able to be tasted, and looking for experiences that brought a smile to my body and allowed rest without judgment. All of these and many more skills allowed me to move with the tentative grace necessary to achieve balance.

I refused to go into a panic. I refused to go into overload. I worked on gratitude and prayer. I explored once again my sense of spiritual connection. I decided to feed and water the positive and the purposeful in my life. To keep my feet firmly in this plane of existence and combat the pain and discomfort with compassion and love. Fight the fight of familiarity.

I would not embrace my pain but comforted the pain. I would not have that experience define me but define my own feelings and self from outside of the experience. Look into the discomfort and embrace my sense of self without the discomfort. Explore, be open, be kind, empathize, yet not grasp onto this single moment as the full expression of myself.

I would not allow Anxiety to flood my body and Fear to dictate my outcome. My survival was coming from the source of love, not Fear.

Only love is real.

CHAPTER THIRTY-TWO

ANXIETY ADDICTION

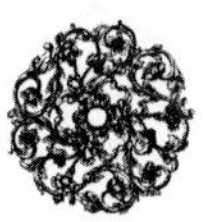

The secret of change is to focus all of your energy, not on fighting the old, but on building the new.

—Socrates

Chemicals spill out and into the space within. They travel long corridors seeking and searching for meaning. They race into our cells and become feelings. We know our thoughts are chemicals released in our body, and then we understand those chemicals as feelings. When they complete the loop back to our brain, we experience emotion.

What happens when we have rehearsed certain feelings and emotions over and over again? When we have flooded our body with the chemicals that put us into fight, flight, or freeze? When we have continued to feed our system the same chemical diet repeatedly, and then we decide to stop? This is called withdrawal.

Our body will become accustomed to the energy and the survival chemicals that our mind continues to make. Scientists have found this in patients who experience acute pain. If an individual experiences enough acute pain, they can create a buildup of electrical signals in the central nervous system (CNS) that overstimulate the nerve fibers.

This effect, known as "windup," is a term compared to a windup toy's buildup of electrical signals. Winding a toy with more intensity leads to the toy running faster for longer. Chronic pain works in the same way, which is why a person can feel pain long after the event that first caused it. In addition, people will continue to feel the pain even though the pain has stopped. This is because the brain continues the chemicals to keep the "norm" of the pain going.

Thoughts, feelings, and behaviors are connected. Chronic pain makes it easy to feel distressed, give up, and become a victim. "Woe is me," "life isn't fair," and other unhelpful thoughts increase one's focus on pain and can make it worse. It fosters Anxiety, anger, frustration, and hopelessness. It leads to what experts call pain catastrophizing—an exaggerated negative response toward actual or anticipated pain.

Enjoying a deep, flavorful cup of coffee every morning as we get into the car and drive in traffic to work, we begin the conditioning of our body. When we deny ourselves the coffee or the stressful drive into the office, we suddenly experience withdrawal. Our body looks for the caffeine and looks for the daily stress. Without our "norm," we feel off. The body is now familiar with this pattern and actually craves caffeine and, strangely enough, the stress. In fact, we can feel the tension even when we are not in a stressful situation. Our body is feeding off the chemicals, being energized by reliving our past stressors.

We can become addicted to stress hormones, just like caffeine. Unfortunately, we have now become addicted to our own thoughts. Breaking the stress or drama of chaos in our lives is where we step out of our past conditioning and into the unknown. This is where we have to decide what we want to feel, who we do want to be, how we break the Fear of the unknown and begin to embrace the uncomfortable.

Anxiety—especially Anxiety attacks—can create what's known as "hypersensitivity." This is when your mind is so in touch with the way your body has felt that it notices every single sensation your body experiences. You then hyper-focus on the sensations to the point where those senses appear to be amplified.

Hypersensitivity is actually one of the main reasons that those with Health Anxiety and panic attacks have trouble curing it without help—"Health Anxiety," a subset of Anxiety and panic attacks, cause individuals to simply "over-notice" everything, and noticing everything causes more Anxiety, making the symptoms worse.

The body holds all of the stress and pain and experiences of the past within it. It holds the chemicals that were released in every cell. These cells replicate over and over, continuing to recreate the same patterns and experiences that are no longer occurring within them. This then becomes an addiction. This becomes what we know as trauma; this becomes the journey back to health.

The good news is our cells do replicate and change regularly. So, each time we reach for something helpful, or something good or a positive experience, this replaces the cell that had the damaging chemicals with the new positive experiences. As we process and release our past pain, we are creating a future that can be beautiful and new. Our bodies work to change our chemistry, and they are continually looking to experience homeostasis. During withdrawal, we may crave the turmoil of drama or Anxiety, but our bodies can be reprogrammed and can be "cleansed" of the chemicals that no longer serve us. Like the cleaning crew, they are ridding us of the trash of the past.

Initially, it feels unfamiliar. Unfamiliar feels uncomfortable. Knowing the past feels comfortable; our bodies will want to experience what it knows. It will look for the stress and pain if this is our past understanding. Yet the unfamiliar allows us to find health in the same way that a woman in an abusive relationship may be frightened and scared of what she does not know. The abuse is familiar, and she may feel like she has some sense of control. She knows what to expect. Yet this doesn't make the situation positive or healthy. It does not mean she should continue. Stepping out into the unknown is challenging, yet the more we allow ourselves to experience different, the different thus becomes the familiar.

The Unfamiliar

Let's say you only go to the same gas station because you're familiar with the station and feel safe at this gas station. The gas station closes while renovating, and you're now forced to go somewhere else. Someplace you do not know, someplace that you feel is sketchy. Your worry level is up the first time you go here. After a month of repeatedly going to the same new station, you have become familiar with the station, the people working there, and the neighborhood. You are comfortable and maybe even feel safe. Now you have two gas stations you can go to. Your world has grown because you have chosen to try something new. You gained information about the place and, most importantly, yourself. You can do different things, and you can try to reach for unfamiliar things and make it familiar.

You have learned to control your worry rather than Fear controlling you; you have learned that stepping into the unfamiliar is not equated with bad. You have begun to reprogram your cells, your body, and you lead the control of your mind and emotions.

Stepping in the direction of Fear does not regain your life. Yet listening to Anxiety reminds us this is how we can break an addiction. Anxiety asks you to step into something new and then decide how you feel. Anxiety does not want you to decide that all things in the future will be the same as the past. This is how you regain your sense of self. This is how you listen to your friend Anxiety.

Notice if Fear is eating away at you, eating your resolve, eating your logic, eating your life path, pulling you from YOU. Fear feeds off of your weakness. Do not give in to it! Do not feed it! If you have to run, run toward that which Fear is telling you not to experience. When there is no saber-tooth tiger, know it's time to run back to the field, gather your berries and talk with those around you. Your people, your support, take in the wind and clouds and the fresh smells of the flowers. Bath in the forest and find that you do have so much to enjoy.

Reach for the good wolf inside. Decide to starve that which is harmful yet familiar. Grow your plant of love, your neural pathways. Decide who you are. Who you want to be and feel, and water your needs. Use your tools to push yourself into the unfamiliar and break the addiction.

Do not hesitate to run into your life before doubt can think you into the past.

CHAPTER THIRTY-THREE

COLD HANDS, COLD FEET

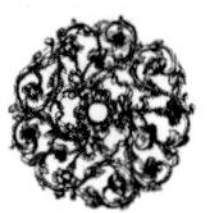

Judge your success by what you had to give up in order to get it.

—Dalai Lama XIV

The sun hasn't yet begun to rise as the ice hits the cooler. It is four in the morning, and my husband is loading dry ice, frozen gloves, socks, snacks, and drinks as if we're packing for a weird picnic.

Cryotherapy is a type of treatment that uses extreme cold. Frozen gloves and socks are worn for ninety minutes, the entire duration of drug infusion—they lessen the drug's ability to move into those areas. This decrease reduces the chance of side effects from the medication on the body's nerve endings.

The blood vessels constrict smaller and smaller with each frozen moment. Numb and prickly, the sense of cold shoots up your hands and feet. Your body decides whether to fire hot or cold neurons as the pain intensifies. Settling into the cold discomfort as your extremities experience a type of hypothermia, the blood vessel constrictions decrease the chemotherapy drug's ability to flow into those nerve endings. This is the use of "cold hands and feet."

Constant firing of the nerves, shooting messages of pain into the body, is one of the side effects of chemotherapy. This nerve damage is known as neuropathy. Neuropathy causes the nerves to fire incorrectly, and patients experience nerve-ending numbness and pain. Chemotherapy can damage nerves that affect feeling and movement in the hands and feet. Doctors call this condition chemotherapy-induced peripheral neuropathy (CIPN). Symptoms can be severe and difficult to exist with, affecting a person's quality of life. Damage to those nerves can affect how the body sends signals to muscles, joints, skin, and internal organs.

One of the ways to bypass the onslaught of chemicals from entering parts of the body is to drop the body temperature down to below sixty-two degrees Fahrenheit. Studies suggest that wearing frozen gloves and socks for ninety minutes during chemotherapy can help control these neuropathy symptoms. However, keeping the gloves and socks frozen for the twelve hours of infusions was a process.

Click, click, click—the cooler wheels would echo as they rolled along the long hospital walkway to the infusion center. Constantly being aware of the time, how much longer to the end of this drug? When will the next one be administered? Monitoring the timing of glove placement and not allowing your hands and feet to feel even slightly comfortable. This was the process necessary for using the gloves and socks during my TCH protocol treatment. The nurses would gown up head-to-toe in personal protective gear and begin the transfusion process. I would gown up with cold/ frozen gloves and socks as well as a hat of ice.

We would need to keep rotating the gloves and socks as they became warm. We hauled dry ice in a cooler to keep the freezing going for eight or more hours each visit. Long, cold days had us leaving at 6:00 a.m. and arriving home around 8:00 p.m. Thank God I had my husband by my side. Thank goodness he was there when I had my allergic reaction. I remember that they had difficulty finding my oxygen level because my hands were so dang cold. They could not even get an oxygen reading.

Working on your physical health can be time-consuming, as is working on your mental health. Having a healthy body without a healthy mind puts us in a place of despair. We can begin to notice that mental health moves our body toward wellness, yet when our body is well and our mind is off, it becomes more challenging to navigate. Then we have the combo of the mind and body affecting each other. How does one reach for the work of being healthy without noticing this duality? How can one embrace a means of moving forward as we encounter the dance of life's challenges?

We all know the mind affects the body and the body affects the mind, for both are interconnected and neither can exist without the other. Where did the difficulty begin? Struggling with this question uses the energy needed to embark upon our journey. Don't get caught in the "chicken or the egg" conversation. Instead, move forward.

CHAPTER THIRTY-FOUR

FEEDING THE GOOD WOLF

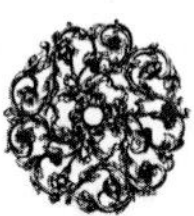

If you have the courage to start, you have the courage to succeed.

—Mel Robbins

Triple positive invasive ductal carcinoma, stage II, measuring 1.5 cm. Estrogen positive, progesterone positive, and Her2 positive. Right breast cancer.

Once I had found my team, I began to work on my plan to resolve my issue, writing out my thoughts and desires and seeing my future. I worked on connecting with the energy all around me and feeling that energy filled with love. Seeing and visualizing myself in the future full of life with my hair blowing in the breeze, laughing, and healthy. Expansive and golden, the positive emotions filled my body and fed my soul.

Speaking these mind movies with words, I wrote out my meditations. I spoke as though these things had already happened. I used "I AM" language. So many of the meditations I found spoke about the future rather than the present. I knew I needed to work in the present. I needed to see myself in the present feeling good, my body healed, and my genes clean. Feel it, be it, own it.

I practiced and meditated and practiced. I got ready for my first chemotherapy session. I was mentally set as I got myself physically set.

Before COVID, masks in place with plastic face shields and disposable gowns, the nurses were swathed head to toe in personal protective gear. Their hands in plastic gloves were placed on top of the gowns. Sealed and protected, they approached me with the medication to put in my body. All of this in case they were to get a little bit of the "medicine" on themselves. The nurse told me the medication would burn their skin and cause horrid reactions. And yet, here they were, placing it directly into my veins. Before COVID, before PPE became a household word, my husband and I experienced the feeling of being in the movie *Outbreak*—a very bizarre reality.

Carboplatin is a mustard-gas derivative. Need I say more? The drug known as Docetaxel, is from the Pacific yew tree, otherwise known as the tree of death. Nearly all parts of the yew tree are considered toxic and poisonous to humans, and it is said that care should be exercised when working with this species. And a drug with the generic name of Trastuzumab, the third medication, is a biological drug that causes heart damage.

I was scheduled for six sessions, spaced out with three weeks in between. I would continue to work and see clients throughout the process and keep to a schedule that felt doable—at times overwhelming, yes—but necessary for me to maintain a sense of self.

Dawn was breaking on the horizon when we went to the hospital for the first time. We gathered all of our items—the cold hands and feet, ice packs, the ice bottles, the snacks, and the frozen coconut-water slushy. The pattern of our visits became established: draw blood, meet with my oncologist, and then head down to the infusion center.

The infusion center was busy. Very busy! A fully dressed pirate wandered into the waiting area—yes, I just said a fully dressed pirate. Telling bad jokes and singing songs, he would volunteer his time to lighten the room's mood. As ridiculous as it may seem, I so appreciated his generosity and corny jokes. I looked forward to him possibly appearing at my visits.

The scale rang out its number, and the blood pressure machine took its measurements as they weighed me, recording each number in my chart with each visit. Warming in the oven were heavy blankets. I would grab one on my way to the fancy recliners with small TVs attached. Attempting to provide comfort and relaxation as best as they could, they would wrap me in blankets and head off to get my cocktail of poison. It was kind of like being in business class on an airplane. Only the cocktails were not so great.

Initially, the chemo reaction seemed horrible yet doable. Eventually, I found that one horrid reaction was due to all the medication they put me on in the hopes of decreasing any problems. Horrendous constipation was a result of these preventative medications. I will never again "poo-poo" those who struggle with constipation. I stopped all those medications and took only the steroids and antihistamines once I finally found some relief.

Everything felt far away, like I was floating around with the world, but not truly in it. It was hard to follow conversations. It wasn't easy to walk for any length of time. I found that I was experiencing what I thought was "chemo brain." I broke out in acne and a rash all over my body. My head was swimming and pounding. Incessant and severe back pain racked my body, radiating down my sides as I struggled with diarrhea. My mouth hurt, and I had a sore throat. The acne started to weep and ooze, and my right collar bone became swollen and retained fluid.

Then it was time for round number two.

We left at dawn yet again and went through the routine. I was sitting in my chair covered with a warm blanket, talking with my nurse, when suddenly everything went awry. Her expression suddenly changed, and my husband stopped talking. They were staring at my face, asking me if I felt all right.

"Yes, I feel fine. Why?"

"You're turning red all over your face, and you have large blotches popping out." The nurse reacted quickly and pulled the plug on the treatment. She ran for a blood pressure cuff, and when she returned, apparently, I looked normal. They checked my blood pressure: 245 over 160. Suddenly, doctors were running, nurses were pumping me full of Diphenhydramine, and everyone went on high alert. Hell, strangely enough, I was allergic to the deadly chemicals they were putting in my body! Huh, who would have thought?

Thank the Lord. *Maybe they will stop? Maybe we could try another type of therapy?*

Augh . . . no.

They pumped me up high on Diphenhydramine, so I felt pretty dang good, and they kept the treatment going, but at half speed. Now it took even longer. Hours turned into more hours. Eventually, the day turned into night, and the staff left. My husband, the nurse, and I closed down the bar.

My doctors added more steroids, more antihistamines, and more medication to take prior to my treatments. This was to help me ward off the allergic reaction and stop me from going into anaphylactic shock. Thankfully it cured my chemo brain and horrible backache, as well and the acne and rash. Those were not normal reactions. Apparently, my blood pressure was so high that I had been dissociating while having allergic reactions all over my body.

I decided with even more conviction that I would not take all of the crazy medications, only those necessary to combat the reactive onslaught of the chemicals they were doing warfare with on me.

I was going to do "love warfare" on my body and them.

CHAPTER THIRTY-FIVE

SIX WEEKS

You don't become what you want, you become what you believe.

—Oprah Winfrey

I had asked for six weeks to eliminate the lump in my breast, and after six weeks, I was again sitting in the doctor's office. I asked them to check the breast to see that it was gone. They smiled and gave an "of course." They checked my breast and could not find anything. I asked them to do an ultrasound. They eventually did—nothing, no lump, no bump, nothing!

I was ecstatic and told them, "See, I did get rid of it!"

They responded, "The treatment is working. You need to keep going forward."

Chemo is hard. It attempts to kill a part of your body in the hopes that your soul will hang on. Well, hang on is what I was going to do. I lost my hair everywhere, including eyelashes and eyebrows. I lost the love of food and the taste that allows it to comfort and swim over my taste buds so they fire in excitement, making me melt inside. I lost my strength and my ability to do all that I wanted. My body grew weaker and weaker, giving way to hurt, pain, and exhaustion. But I did not lose my resolve.

Resolve was still there, and it would not die. My sense of self and knowing that I was all right, even if the doctors couldn't see it, was alive and kicking. It kept me going through the chemo, through the surgery, through the radiation, and allowed me to push to an early end of the Trastuzumab treatment. Trastuzumab damages your heart muscle; this medication has a known history of creating heart failure. So much so that the doctors have to check your heart regularly to make sure that the muscle has not been too severely damaged. They would schedule echocardiograms to monitor the damage placed on the muscle that keeps all of us alive.

I kept my resolve to remember my health, my truth, myself. And then, I was done. It was over. I had lost the possibility of a new office and our beloved current office in the process. I had lost my hair, strength, sense of taste, and a breast, but I was still here, and my vision was clear. I once again walked the path I talk of with my clients. I did my work. I did my meditations. I went to the acupuncturist, recharged my batteries, and focused on myself. I did my art and used it to motivate me to bigger and larger aspects of love in my life. I reached out to those who I loved and let them know I cared for them deeply. I appreciated the little things and the big ones. I visited with friends and laughed. I hugged and smiled and decided that I was going to live well, not die badly.

And then COVID-19 hit.

CHAPTER THIRTY-SIX

SELF-CARE

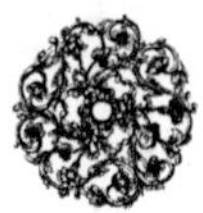

If you can't control your mind, everything and everyone else will.

—Dr. Joe Dispenza

Why no one seemed to know that COVID was coming amazes me. I mean, the entire world was getting sick. Eight hundred people in Italy died in ONE DAY, for god's sake. Personally, I started "acquiring" masks from the hospital in February. I went to the grocery store and got supplies in April. What were these people doing? It is a virus with no cure, and it knows no race, color, land, politics, or age. COVID doesn't care. I know I tend to think the worst. I have Anxiety, damn it. But really?!

So, the powers that be decided to see if they could stop the spread and asked each person to care and show love and kindness. Stay home and spread love, not COVID. Show you care about your neighbor and keep the virus's ability to spread to a minimum by wearing a mask. Do not give the virus a host, a place to live and grow. Kill it by starving it—do not feed it, do not allow it to thrive. Starve the bad wolf, feed love and compassion instead. Attempt to decrease its ability to expand so our health care is not overwhelmed. Put it in the dark and keep it far away from us.

It did not work. It kept spreading. Staying home was too difficult. People were unable to sustain their businesses and their way of life. People pushed back. Republicans said, "We will make a vaccine and get back to normal." Democrats said, "How are you protecting us till this happens?" But Fear created its own narrative: "It is not a virus; it is political." Fear started to gain ground—yes, the "all-powerful" aspect of Fear. The one emotion we know will pull us offline and produce Anxiety. For only when Fear is talking to us about things that are not in our best interest does Anxiety rear its head.

Remember, when Fear pulls us away from our best selves, our Anxiety goes through the roof. When we do not have appropriate Fear, we have natural consequences—death at the tiger's paw. In the United States, Fear became politicized for personal and political gain, and I saw Anxiety go into overdrive as an entire nation became gripped in a battle of hope versus Fear. Of course, Anxiety was doing its best to get us to pay attention. But as COVID-19 came closer and closer to each of us, Fear soared.

There are still those who wish to continue to spread Fear to their advantage. My job became one where people had to be reminded of what skills had worked for them: Looking at the unknown with an open mind, becoming familiar with an unfamiliar situation. Take this time as an opportunity to pause, an opening to reevaluate who they were, what they truly wanted, how they wanted to feel, become curious. Notice how much they appreciated that which they initially thought they could not tolerate. Open themselves up to new possibilities as they suddenly found themselves doing what they had NOT done before: sitting at home with themselves.

I worked with them to find ways to be in their lives. What brought meaning to them? How to stay connected even at a distance. How to better their mind and their body. How to be creative and express their emotions in ways they could appreciate.

What was their structure to the day? How did they enjoy their own space? How could they connect to nature and enjoy this world around us? I helped them find a sense of purpose for the day, week, and months—goals, steps, self.

Working on self-care is very new to anxious people. They tend to be pleasers, helpers, or hyper-focused on judging themselves. This leads to a need to perform. For those with Anxiety, self-care often is equated with selfish behavior. Understanding the difference can be a long process.

Self-focus is not self-care. Remember that Anxiety—especially Anxiety attacks—can create what's known as "hypersensitivity." This is when your mind is so in touch with the way your body feels that it notices every single sensation your body experiences and focuses on it to the point where the sensation appears to be amplified. Focus on the body means the body is in charge and the mind is not.

Hypersensitivity and self-focus are actually one of the main reasons that those with Health Anxiety notice everything, causing more Anxiety and making the symptoms worse. Self-focus is the opposite of self-care.

Self-care is not selfish behavior. Clients have often been taught that taking care of themselves is selfish. This is not so. Selfish behavior is when one is taking something away from someone else for your own benefit or desire. For example, eating all the dinner so no one else can have any is selfish. Deciding someone else's life doesn't matter because it is an inconvenience to you—that is selfish. We see this in movies where the plotline exposes how people will decide that they deserve to live at the expense of others.

When we take away from others, this is the definition of selfish. Yet, when we care for ourselves, we allow others the opportunity to better themselves. Suddenly, others are not held responsible for caring for us at their own expense. Now everyone can reap their own sense of accomplishment and rewards. With self-care, we are adding to our life, not subtracting from ourselves or others.

When we care for ourselves, we become happier, and suddenly, those we care about are happier, more open, or doing the things we have wanted them to do forever with no success. In addition, our self-care opens others up to the opportunity to also feel confident, successful, or free to pursue their own wants. It is only when we take care of ourselves that these opportunities open. I call it "the magic."

The first aspect of self-care is to stop terrorizing yourself. Don't take a scary situation and make yourself worse by imagining worst-case scenarios. Building negative aspirations and possibilities only push us into overload. What happens is that we play out the scenario and end it at the worst place and then don't go past this into the future. We play the thought up to the worst possible situation over and over again until we are in a frenzy and have made ourselves miserable.

For example, "I'm going to be alone if my spouse leaves me. I will be sad and alone and scared." This is where we typically end. We play this over and over again until we are the only person who has made us feel this way—no one else.

Here's a better way to play out a future-case scenario:

> *If my spouse leaves me, I will be sad and alone and scared, and I will have to go to work and make some money. I will get to know more people at work. I may make new friends and meet new people. I may meet someone and go on a date. The more I go out, the more I will learn about myself and others. This can help me understand what I want. I may grow and learn how to set limits and boundaries or ask for my needs to be met. I may then find someone who appreciates me and what I value. That person may continue be in my life, and I can learn to support them as they support me.*

This is the ending Fear does not want you to consider or want you to experience. If you do, you will not be feeding and nurturing Fear. You will not be enhancing and adding to Fear. You will be KNOWING. You will be venturing into curiosity and gathering your own information, not feeding Fear.

Make a vow *not* to terrorize yourself. This seems simple, but notice how often you may do this. Try and love yourself enough to stop scaring yourself with worse-case scenarios and life's "what ifs." Instead, try self-care rather than self-scare.

Those with Anxiety often find they need to help everyone except themselves. *I need to be kind to other people, but not to myself. Others do not need to earn love, but I do. Others should not hate themselves, but I do. I will be horrible, mean, judging, and demanding of myself. I will hate on myself and do so over and over again with my thoughts.*

This is not self-care. Some feel they need to take bubble baths and shop, but the ultimate self-care is controlling our own ability to be understanding, loving, and gentle, combined with curiosity and the repetition of stepping into life. These actions bring about positive growth in ourselves and those we love.

So, what is self-care? Self-care means being kind, patient, and gentle to yourself. This is often the way we treat others. But remember, you are also a part of "others." Self-care is mourning what we did not receive. Acknowledging the abuses, accepting the sadness, and the losses so we may recognize our needs. It is not about ruminating on loss. It is not rehearsing that which we did not get, but an opportunity to start the healing recognition of what we deserve. It's working on the anger we experienced and were not allowed to express—the sadness we felt and then were told we were too sensitive. It may include visiting the events or shifting the old feelings with hypnotherapy or brainspotting and being allowed to speak up for ourselves, say what we did not get a chance to say, or visualize moving forward in non-abusive ways. We thus become the person who has our own back, standing up for ourselves. This allows us to work on recognizing that others are not the answer, but it is reconnecting with self that heals.

Others cannot heal our past hurts or fears. Self-care is dropping the expectation that our loved ones will fix us, make us whole, or that we are somehow broken. They cannot change the past or undo the hurt. But we can work on parenting ourselves. We can move to a place of forgiveness and self-forgiveness for our human imperfections, allowing us to make healthier choices in our own relationships with ourselves, friends, and partners.

Every cell in your being has learned that letting go and moving on is painful, yet when opened to the experience, it also learns that moving from connection to disconnection back to connection is the growth we have been searching for. We learn to see the Fear and Anxiety of not healing is bigger and more painful than the actual process of nurturing ourselves. This new beginning creates a positive challenge. It empowers us. We can learn to be safe, secure, and alone or with another. Others are no longer the means to our own health. We are.

Work on remembering to build yourself up versus tearing yourself down. Step into an act of self-kindness as you support yourself through the grief of what you did not receive. Self-blame, guilt, judgment, perfectionism, entitlement, or ignoring this pain is the opposite of kindness. Build yourself up and try to praise yourself. Notice when and how you have done something nice or well. Recognize your accomplishments and acknowledge your successes.

You are born with worth. This worth cannot be added to or taken away. You have just as much potential and worth as you had when you were born. What we do can add to others' lives, but not our own worth. We can allow others to experience a sense of love and self-appreciation, but how often do we appreciate ourselves? How often do we nurture ourselves? How often do we let the old die and regrow? How do we let our needs be fulfilled by ourselves before we reach for another to enhance their needs?

Notice I said others can *enhance* our needs; they do not *give* us our needs or *maintain* our needs, for we have the ability to sit under our own vine, under our own fig tree, and no one will make us afraid (Micah 4:4).

CHAPTER THIRTY-SEVEN

STRUCTURE

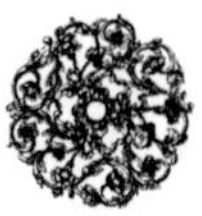

Knowing there is structure, hidden or felt, to the random gives pleasure.

—Cecil Balmond

We were still taken by surprise when told to stay at home in March. "Shelter in place, move into safety, be understanding, help your neighbor," and watch from afar as Fear entered our lives. And then we heard the dreaded words: toilet paper.

People started to buy ammunition and make runs on grocery stores, grabbing and stockpiling anything they could get their hands on. Like *Terminator 2: Judgment Day*, Sarah Conner opens her hidden cache of supplies filled with weapons and, instead, roll after roll of toilet paper is displayed within. Of course, at our house, being the Anxiety Gal, we were already set. We did not have Sarah's cache, but I had gathered supplies, and we had toilet paper for the people who would be living at our house, and the pantry was stocked full.

There is a difference between being prepared and acting with Fear. We were not looking at this as a scary event but as an opportunity to care for each other, enjoy our family, and brace for the unknown. Did others have toilet paper, did they need paper, could we supply them toilet paper? What did we need to care for the household and our friends? What type of food, activities, connections, exercises, games, books, movies, face protection, air purifiers could we gather so we could relax? Our unknown was not filled with Fear but offered us a chance to advance into exploration, creativity, and growth. We gathered those we loved close to us. We took time to respect each person's needs and space. Our home was ready. We had seven people who were settling down for our time together, moving in and around each other like a well-greased carousel.

Easter came early, and the Easter Bunny brought puzzles, candy, and a sizeable geometric picture that we worked on coloring and creating as our map of connection throughout the wee hours of the night. Each morning we would awake and find the image closer to completion. The children worked together, talking, sharing, as laughter reverberated throughout the home. There was no sense of Fear within our house, but a profound understanding of working on encouragement, a depth of feeling as our sense of kindred spirit was cultivated.

We used our time to share stories, understand each other more deeply, explore who we were, and enjoy the sense of warmth and acceptance. Like bathing in a warm tub, we relaxed into self-care and waited.

Anxiety started to grow among my clients. Those who had traumatic histories were most affected. It brought back an understanding that control is an illusion and the possibility of loss and lack. It threw them back into triggered reactions preceding their newly instilled responses to the unknown.

Patients fell into the fog of Fear and ran around grabbing anything they could. They found themselves once again living in scarcity. A world filled with want, with no love, acceptance, safety, or support. Instead, they were thrown into a past of feeling competition, lack, and abuse. Yet, I offered up how COVID was summoning a new opportunity for their inner work to mature. COVID challenged them to cultivate new behaviors, thoughts, and produce unique outcomes. It pushed them to enhance their work on their process.

I reminded each patient that structure would help. I encouraged them to decide how they wanted to envision each day and how they imagined themselves. We worked on how to experience and explore ways to ensure that they would and could continue to have this structure in their lives. We worked on four pillars of stability. I explored with each person their vision of these aspects and where they may need more support. Like a table with four legs, when one leg becomes unstable or broken, the table can still stand with three legs. We worked on maintaining their stability and how they could continue to build each leg.

In the case of one client, they worked to open past programming and fill it with new prospects. We would sit and explore the gaslighting experienced around their own possibilities and how an imaginary world had been created that they blindly accepted and followed. Through their process, they understood and saw that others were directing their experiences and their understanding. They started to see how they believed the nonsense, how they continued to gaslight themselves and maintain this delusion. They began to embody a sense of their own. They started to understand how they could mentally recreate and change their beliefs of life and self around their own truth rather than the misinformation of themselves created by others. How to blend their thoughts, feeling and actions toward self-awareness. To sit with the discomfort and not push their friend Anxiety away. How to become and embrace the uncomfortable feelings within themselves rather than to bend others to fit their old patterns.

For many, it felt like their legs were being destroyed. They were unstable like a broken table. But we were together. We worked as a team. Challenges allow us to grow, change, choose more, and choose differently. COVID pushed us.

Our world was crashing around us—not 2.5 thousand, but 5.7 million people had passed away. We needed to walk away from past programming into something new, filled with possibilities.

We needed to work on our table legs.

MIRACLE EIGHT

CHAPTER THIRTY-EIGHT

RECONSTRUCTION

Discomfort is the currency of your dreams.

—Brooke Castillo

Finally, my silver lining had arrived. After having my muscles repeatedly sliced apart from three C-sections, my oncology surgeon said she would remove fat from my stomach to place in my breast. She would then perform a tummy tuck at the same time. I was ecstatic! Finally, something nice for me. I was looking forward to regaining my physical shape after all my body had endured.

Radiation was only twenty seconds. Twenty seconds every single day for weeks. Check-in and undress. Sit till you're called. Make small talk till the machine moved and groaned in patterns above your body. Rotating and pulsing as you absorbed more poison into the system, positioned the same way each and every time.

Radiation therapy works by damaging cells and destroying the genetic material that controls how cells grow and divide. While both healthy and cancerous cells are damaged by radiation therapy, it aims to eliminate as few normal cells as possible. As a result, healthy cells reportedly will repair and divide, cancerous cells will not. It was only for a few moments, but the effects continue for months, if not years.

Placing my arms above my head, I would find the preformed grooves of the molds for my body. I was positioned in these molds to hold me in place. Then the radiation would begin to bombard me. Radiation attacked my cells, good ones and bad ones. They caused my muscles to shorten, constrict, and pull inward. It caused my skin to wither and harden, shrinking my breast ever further.

During surgery, they removed the "non-lump" because maybe there was still one cancerous cell remaining. They took out lymph nodes where there had never been any cancer. Prior to surgery, they stuck a needle into my nipple without any anesthesia. The syringe was filled with dye, and then they press and push it around to move it into my nodes.

"We are going to stick a needle into one of the most tender and sensitive parts of your body."

"No, you will not get any numbing agents or anesthesia."

"Now we will mash and press and push that sensitive part till you want to scream."

UGH! Over and over, they mashed and pushed and traumatized my breast, visit after visit, so they can now bombard me with radiation? Really? In fact, using cancer-causing methods for cancer diagnosis and treatment seems counterintuitive to me.

But what do I know? I am not a doctor. What we do know is that ionizing radiation, while very useful, is classified as a human carcinogen. It can damage cells and DNA, and while used to treat cancer, it is also a known cause of cancer. I would think if men had to have their privates smashed multiple times, then x-rayed, and then use no anesthesia to shoot themselves full of dye, things may be different.

The surgeon said the lumpectomy would be minor, and it would not be very noticeable. They removed half of my right breast; it was healthy tissue with no cancer to be found as the original lump was gone. In fact, when they did a biopsy of the lumpectomy tissue, they found no cancerous cells, none. Yay me!

But they still pushed for radiation.

So, when I was told they would do a tummy tuck—YES! The surgery would not only remove fat to place into my breast, but they would also remove the excess skin and tissue created from multiple pregnancies. My surgeon also worked on closing up my expanded and torn abdominal muscles. Like a handmade quilt, she worked to close up the gaps and strengthen the walls. She later told me my abdominal muscles were so far apart that no number of sit-ups would ever have rectified the problem.

Sigh . . . So good. I was very excited.

CHAPTER THIRTY-NINE

TABLE LEGS

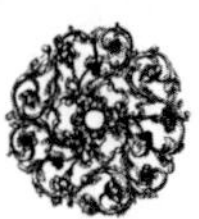

Life is change, change is stability.

—Zen Proverb

Structure in our lives allows us to maintain a steadfast resolve providing support and a binding essence to our mental health. Strong, secure, ever fast, we can attach ourselves to these pillars when the winds blow and the world turns upside down. I equate these mental health pillars to the legs of a table. When we have a table with four sturdy legs, we can stand on our table and feel the support underneath us. Well built, sturdy and rugged, if one leg gives out, we still have three legs to support us, allowing us time to fix the broken leg. If two legs give out, there is still a possibility the table can hold. But if we only have one leg in place, collapse and possible disaster ensue.

Active engagement in building and maintaining these legs is a large part of how we diligently work on therapy and ourselves. The legs may, at some point, break, become worn out, or need replacing, but if we have worked to establish each one, our stress level will not overwhelm us, and we can learn to reach for resiliency. These table legs allow us to rebuild the loss, reestablish stability, and move through the storms of life.

Here is my brief description of each of the four main legs for one's table: mental, growth, behavior, and social.

Mental

We have covered many ways to rewire and establish our thoughts. Yet we also know that our body requires the proper nutrition to work efficiently and help us to balance and feel secure. Thus, our mental leg includes options such as choosing new ways to think, building brain muscle through meditation, and finding balance with food and/or medication. So much is now known about our stomachs and the brain-gut connection. We know that the happiness neurotransmitters of dopamine, GABA, and serotonin are produced in our brains and bellies. Although serotonin is well known as a brain neurotransmitter, many may not know it is estimated that ninety percent of the body's serotonin is made in the digestive tract.

In fact, altered levels of this peripheral serotonin have been linked to diseases, such as irritable bowel syndrome, cardiovascular disease, and osteoporosis. This work was published in an article titled, "Indigenous Bacteria from the Gut Microbiota Regulate Host Serotonin Biosynthesis," from Caltech. We know that serotonin and dopamine play a crucial role in maintaining homeostasis in the human body. Studies on these neurotransmitters have primarily revolved around their role in the fight-or-flight response, transmitting signals across a chemical synapse and nutritional absorption. Keeping our health and nutrition in balance allows us to balance our bodies and our minds.

Ensuring that you are eating healthy foods and actively caring for your stomach and intestines by monitoring the types of food you eat, your weight, fat intake, and engaging in eating a variety of foods will help your body and mental stability work to support you.

Growth

Finding ways to grow is another leg to our table. Each person needs to actively look for ways to be creative, find meaning, purpose, and add learning into their lives. Engaging in artistic endeavors, such as painting, drawing, cooking, writing, or photography, are ways we can learn to once again play in our daily lives. Learning to complete puzzles, video games, word searches, expanding our brains and developing new connections, is essential for healthy living.

Growth can also include contributing to others through giving, becoming involved in civic activities, groups, or our own families. Growing with others opens a sense of purpose and meaning, even if that growth is with another living entity such as a garden. Gardening and connecting to the ground expands our creativity and helps us with our behaviors. There is increasing evidence that exposure to plants and green space, particularly to gardening, is beneficial to mental and physical health, helping us grow creatively, physically, and mentally. Planting trees and adding to nature provides us a sense of purpose, while it also decreases the stress placed on our earth.

Behavior

Movement improves our mental health by reducing Anxiety, depression, and disconnection by improving our cognitive function while alleviating symptoms such as low self-esteem and social withdrawal. Thus, behavior is an important leg to our table of stability. Our behavior is related to physical activity—moving, exploring, and seeking out the familiar and unfamiliar. Even though it may not be physically straining, moving with exploration and curiosity is essential. Researchers have found that physical activities play a powerful role in strengthening self-worth and confidence.

Physical activity or exercise is a leg of our table. Exercise is a natural and effective anti-Anxiety treatment. It relieves tension and stress, boosts physical and mental energy, and enhances well-being. We know that physical activity helps to relax the muscles and align the body and the mind in a place of health, purpose, and meaning. Studies have shown that you can actually help your nervous system become "unstuck" and begin to move out of the immobilization stress response with exercise. Exercise decreases inflammation within the body and stomach, allowing for our happy hormones such as serotonin, dopamine, and GABA to be released. Our physical behavior can promote exploration and connection with ourselves.

Sherri L. Mitchell (Weh'na Ha'mu Kwasset), a lawyer and climate activist, wrote in *Pop-Up Magazine*'s "Year in Search: the search for why" that people spent more time outside during the pandemic exploring the world around them because they could not spend time with people. They explored spaces, woods, fields, pathways, and connected with the presence of others—trees, plants, and animals. Even though they might not have realized it, they were connecting, and they knew they craved connection.

The term known as "forest bathing" is the practice of immersing yourself in nature in a mindful way, using your senses to derive a whole range of benefits for your physical, mental, emotional, and social health. Research has shown molecules released from trees, known as phytoncides, are good for our immunity—it can lessen days of illness, increase recovery from injury or surgery, improve heart and lung health, and increase focus, concentration, and memory. This type of connection helps us to experience an understanding of emotional regulation and understand that we are part of something bigger than ourselves. We learn to ground ourselves in our bodies and our spirit. When we touch the ground, we feel this, and it is one reason why we use the term "grounding" in therapy.

Grounding can be found in meditation as it activates muscles to encounter the present, noticing we are in charge of our thinking and providing us choice to combat the disinformation of Fear. As we connect to self and the energy of the world around us, we recognize that we are not alone. Allowing us to grow and reach for what we know. A deep knowledge of connecting and being with others runs through us as we reach for a higher consciousness: cooperation vs. competition. We can connect physically in so many ways.

SOCIAL

Connection with self and others lends itself to the improvement of our final table leg. Searching for ways to expand kindness in our lives and to those around us is the essence of social connection. As Winston Churchill stated, "We make a living by what we get, but we make a life by what we give." Each expansion increases our ability to receive and provide support. Psychologists and other mental health professionals often talk about the importance of having a strong social support network. They know studies have repeatedly shown that these relationships relieve stress and decrease maladaptive behaviors. Accepting support can come in many ways.

Knowing others are there to back you up emotionally when you need it or offering a shoulder to cry on to someone you care for may be ways we receive or give support. There are also times when we might need a hot meal when we are sick or receive a ride when our car is in the shop. This is known as instrumental support. Lastly, ensuring we have the means to procure informational support for ourselves and for others is also necessary. Information such as guidance, advice, and mentoring helps us connect with others and assists us as we grow into part of our support system.

Once we have established our table legs, we are better able to withstand the many stressors in our lives with a sense of grace and support. Yet maintaining them is essential. We need to constantly add friends, create new ways to explore and play, and find purpose. Connect with our bodies and others while exploring the world around us, and be still and breathe in the essence of self as we age and grow. We have many aspects leaving and entering our lives in a constant flow of change. Because the only constant is change. Embrace it and explore it.

Be curious, step into life, and create your table!

CHAPTER FOURTY

MOVEMENT, NOT LOSS

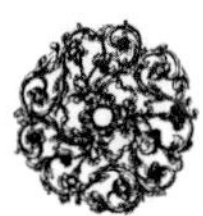

I do remember and then when I try to remember, I forget.
—Winnie the Pooh

I was at home when the embolism occurred. Pain scorched up my leg and groin—extreme, unyielding, and relentless. Yet none of this is in my memory. The event was oppressive and intense. Blocked out and replaced by my brain with a wonderful, blank, soft sense of calm and blurring. Synchronistic, like a beautiful piece of music, each instrument, person, and situational development falling into place added to the beauty of concurrence. When I revisit the event, though traumatic, it aligned beautifully allowing me to still be here. When I step back and take in how the pieces hailed; the sound is beautiful.

Heat and sweat began weeping down my body. Agitated and disturbed, creeping from my head down, the sensations heightened as I asked my husband to get me a cool washcloth.

"Are you okay? Natalie, Natalie! Can you hear me?"

I appeared unresponsive. Lost in my head and not in the world around me.

Suddenly, I came to, awakening from the suspension within.

"Oxygen," I whispered from my lips. Dead-straight eyes, deep and lost.

I couldn't breathe. Gasping, heaving, and fighting for breath, I started to convulse, massive body-wrenching convulsions. Spasms contorted my body as they rocked me physically and massively into severely misshaped dimensions as foam seeped from my mouth. My husband reached for the phone, frantically dialing 911.

My body kept fighting, throwing itself around. The bruising on my neck was black, blue, yellow, and purple. Deep colors of life as I refused to leave. Terrified, my husband rolled me onto my side, attempting to hold me steady until the paramedics arrived.

The paramedics who had just responded to another call were pulling into the station when they responded. Sirens howling the noise grew closer and closer, announcing their assistance and the need for urgency. The paramedics approached the house and bolted upstairs. Pulling me down to the front door, they strapped me into the stretcher. No pulse. No response. No vitals. Here is where I crashed the first time. I was dead before I left the house.

It takes over twenty minutes to arrive at our local hospital when we drive quickly. The paramedics flew! They were unsure as to the amount of time I was legally dead. But they knew it was no less than nine minutes. Once we had arrived, they moved me into emergency, where they were able to shock me back to life, but only for a moment. Once again, they worked to "resurrect" me, yet this would not hold. Once again, my body was failing and fighting and jumping from the table even with the straps holding me into place. In the midst of the noise, yelling, chaotic, symbiotic in a fluid movement, an aggressive young doctor took charge. He was a pulmonologist on call at the emergency room and willing to step out of the normal bounds into possibility.

Thankfully, my oncology team provided us an oncology nurse navigator whom I lovingly referred to as my "mother"—

always there to help me remember what medications I was taking. She knew what my concerns were and would bring them up each visit with every new doctor I met. Before each appointment, she would check to see how I was doing, accompany me to meet with any new doctor, and brought with her over thirty years of health and psychosocial care to my disposal. She was indispensable.

I was in my early forties when I lost my birth mother. Passing away unexpectedly, her death was heart-wrenching and eye-opening in many ways. It allowed me to realize how I grieved, how others grieved, how long love lasted, how I was able to respond positively and devastatingly to trauma. This tragic moment allowed my skills to enhance as I moved into my process and reached for those people important to me—reaching for my table legs.

Now, I was blessed to have my "oncology mother" available for my husband, my team, and myself the night of the embolism. My husband called her directly, and she answered her phone. Arguing, explaining, fighting, she helped the emergency team put all the pieces in place around my history, my needs, my challenges. She had followed me through each appointment, each surgical event, chemotherapy, and cardiac visit. She had information that transcended all of my doctor's, providing a full picture for the emergency staff. She was an unmovable force when there were pushbacks. She navigated and directed our needs for us, ensuring all barriers fell away as she became our angel.

A pulmonary embolism is a big deal, being both common and dangerous. It is dangerous because almost a quarter of pulmonary embolism cases present as sudden death, and up to a third of pulmonary embolisms will ultimately be fatal. For those that survive the embolism, there is the possibility of decreased life expectancy and the development of complications that can impair the quality of life. For this reason, it's critical to make sure that the embolism is correctly diagnosed and properly managed, as that can make all the difference.

My new "mother" was able to keep me safe and was there for my family and for me. Fighting for us, she did not back down when we needed her. I am so very, very thankful for her and her strength.

My husband was with me, the paramedics available and actively in motion, the empty night streets devoid of traffic, the young aggressive doctor who made a quick and accurate diagnoses in the emergency room, and the staff willing to do whatever they could, in addition to my "mother," working all in construct. Each piece added to a synchronistic melody being built and played for me. Profound, intense, and ever-present, it filled our lives. An energetic vibration of sound and waves filling the space between each living moment and being. Yet my heart, stomach, brain, nervous system, lungs, bowels, immune system—all were at risk because of the stress caused by oxygen loss. When your body thinks you are in a place of threat, it needs to protect you. Only I could reset the system and work on correcting this information.

When I awoke, I knew that it was up to me to redirect and correct the direction things were moving. I knew I needed to fight and grow from this experience and use it so others could see and experience their own possibility, to find their own cobbled path.

The synchronistic inevitability that I am still here is a miracle.

CHAPTER FORTY-ONE

THE JAILHOUSE

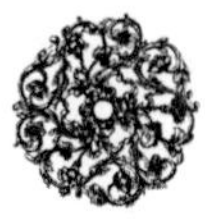

Step up. Don't wait for someone to ask you.

—Reese Witherspoon

Imagine a jail cell. It is cold and scary, and all you can think about is getting out. You are inside alone, with no power, controlled by others, with limited options. Unfortunately, this is where most of us live. Feeling trapped in a mask, a job, or a loveless life known not to be our truth. A pretend life creates a jail where no one sees the real you. Either too afraid to let others know who you are or what you are experiencing, you may continue to punish yourself for circumstances you had no power over. Abandoned by yourself, unwilling and scared to do something different, you are trapped in a horrid existence.

Initially, enhancing our own needs and not looking for others to meet our needs may seem counterintuitive. Understanding that we are loved no matter what and that we will have support, even if only from our own selves, rather than go through life with our needs diminished or dashed into the ground, may be new to us. We can ask for help rather than aim for unreasonable "perfection" from ourselves or others. This is what we tend not to do. Yet we will tell ourselves that others must give us this understanding. They have to tell us that we are loved. They should say what we deserve. They are in charge. They must do this. We know we did not receive our divine birthright: worth, love, and acceptance of who we are, in addition to the freedom to explore and make mistakes without judgment.

So, because I did not get these needs met, "Others need to make me right. They need to do it for me."

Anytime we place our power in another's hands, they will most likely screw it up. Why? Because they are flawed humans. Just like us, they have been hurt, have their own wants and needs, and may even feel alone or misunderstood.

The Guard Is in Charge

Here in the jail, a guard walks outside, each step echoing in the distance, hollow and forlorn. You hope the guard will see you, speak what you deserve, say that they know you need to be loved, understand what you have experienced. You hope and expect this guard will say the magic word that will open your cell. Open the door to freedom and possibility, to love and compassion. Flood you with a rainbow of color that imbibes each building block within. If the guard truly cares for you and wants what is best for you, they will know it and use it, allowing you to experience happiness.

The guard peers through the bars and struggles—struggles to find your word, the magic key. The key that will open the cell so you feel your needs are met, providing you the experience of rainbow-enhanced energy and vibration. Suddenly, the guard finds it! The key is uncovered.

So much joy and excitement radiates from you as you recognize they have used your key. Seeing the happiness within you, the guard keeps utilizing the key in order to keep the cell door open, for it requires consistency. Over and over, they use the key, the unique words, steady, dependable, yet taxing. After a while, the guard becomes tired and doesn't say your special word as much. They have said it so much! Why don't you remember what they said? Why does someone else have to be in charge of your key? All the responsibility for your happiness lies outside of you. It is exhausting for the guard. They need a break. They are worn out. They have kept going for so long now they need to meet their own needs. Maybe the guard is sick. Maybe they are mad. Maybe they have more to do at work. Maybe they are just having a bad day. Maybe, maybe, maybe . . .

You become resentful. Growing inside, the resentment pulsates with concern. It seems like the guard doesn't care; it is as though they have been lying to you. Why are they not taking care of you? Why have they changed? Will they no longer feed you your word and be in charge of your key? You yell at them, and they become upset.

Exhausted, hurt, and overwhelmed, the guard decides they will not use the key so that you can feel their burnout, their pain. But all you feel is loss and rejection. You realize they have the power, and you have none. Once again, you have given all the power to someone else. You have stepped into a pattern. More than likely an old habit that ensures your needs are not met.

You Are in Charge

Let's work this in a different direction.

You are in a cell—cold, scared, alone, struggling—and all you can think about is getting out. You feel trapped in a mask, job, or life that you know is not your truth. A pretend life, a place where no one has seen the real you because you have been too afraid to let others know who you are, scared they will judge you, see you for damaged goods, the vulnerability underneath. Feeling desolate and collared by depression and Anxiety—a horrid jail of existence—you know what your key is.

We have a need to feel love and acceptance. To know love is out in the world. You know what your key is, and then YOU reach for it. Not the guard, but you. You use your key. You say the magic words. You understand what you need to hear. You send compassion and caring to enhance yourself, accepting who you are without judgment. The door swings open, and there is the guard walking their solitary journey. Your eyes connect with theirs, and the guard adds to your existing key, growing it more significant so it becomes difficult for you to lose and forget. They add to but do not control the key. They enhance your experience, but you decide when to open your door. You can open your door or close your door. In or out, out or in, you have total control. The guard does not become exhausted but becomes invigorated by your movement, your ability to care for yourself. Watching you care for your needs propels them to do the same and share their success with you.

The guard enjoys you and your freedom but feels no overwhelming responsibility to keep you propped up and going. They know they are adding to your experience, and you are adding to theirs as they are allowed to explore their own needs and work on their own key. They now cannot use your key to hurt you because you are in charge of your key, no one else. You have control of your own experience. You are now empowered; you have not given your power to someone else. No one can deny you or remove your freedom. Your worth is now your own.

Be aware of your *shoulds* and *musts*. Manners and values help us live together in a society where we can feel comfortable with familiarity, but insults, shaming, and scare tactics are forms of abuse that allow old patterns to be reinforced. Ask yourself, are you becoming the *should*-er, or the abuser, to yourself? Are we our own jailer? Have we picked up on the ways of our culprits? There are those in our past who may have hurt us, but are we continuing the same methods that we know were damaging, shaming, and controlling? Are we lying to ourselves about not needing a key? Not being worthy of a key? That we cannot have a key? Are we continuing the lies of the past?

Can we forgive ourselves and the hurt we have continued to inflict as we move forward into an unfamiliar place of kindness and understanding? Can we move to a place that at first may not be comfortable but reveals for us something new, open, filled with possibilities?

David Richo, a psychotherapist, teacher, and writer, says, "Fear lurks in the shadow of our ego." It is a part of us that wants approval, conformity, and loss of our uniqueness. Whereas fearlessness that is aligned with our values "is our personal and unique potential." Fearlessness opens us up to change, goals, and insight. It can be scary, as it is new and unfamiliar. This unfamiliar place can be uncomfortable. Yet the breaking of this cycle opens us and awakens us.

When we step to the edge, into *impossible,* we step into *I'm possible.* We awaken internally and spiritually. We see two worlds intersecting as our truth is revealed. This new truth, this new understanding, is breaking the ego as we rebuild into ourselves. Fearless is stepping away from the lies and the self-gaslight sayings that "we do not deserve" or "we're not good enough." Instead, we can open up to the divine and understand the power of self-truth and faith.

We can open our cell door and reach for self-care with therapy.

How do we battle that which is not real? With that which is.

CHAPTER FORTY-TWO

I AM DRIVING THE BOAT

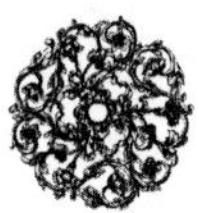

Be miserable. Or motivate yourself. Whatever has to be done, it's always your choice.

—Wayne Dyer

It seems so easy, yet I am hitting my face as the fork moves toward my mouth. *Damn.* The tines poke into me once again, so I must be off course. Eating is impossible. I keep missing my mouth, and holding a fork seems a massive event that my brain can't wrap my head around. It takes so long to move the food while attempting to hold a fork. I end up trying to move my mouth toward the food rather than my hands toward my mouth.

Yes, could you please feed me? I don't seem to work.

Each movement is so big in effort. Struggling to have my brain connect to my body as each thought unravels before it hits the nerves. All I want is to hold my coffee, sit on the toilet, and have a moment of solitude. Not going to happen. I remember a military pilot saying to me, "If you can have coffee and a shit, it's a good day." Hallelujah! I do get it.

There are tubes and connections and no ability to control the coffee mug. Bringing the coffee to my mouth? Too tricky.

Breathe and drink? Umm . . . possible, if I go slowly and deliberately. Being alone? Ha! No one will let me sit by myself because I can't. They give me the "wonder weenie" used in hospitals so individuals can relieve themselves while in bed! Augh! So horrible! But I can't lift myself onto a bedpan even if I wanted to. I can't roll over. I can't move my hands, let alone my body. I'm on an oxygen machine. My voice is breathy and barely able to be heard. But I can wiggle my toes, I can think, I can ask questions quietly given time, I can see and smell and hear what is being said.

This is not what I envisioned. Everything is difficult. It is slow. I am slow. Am I broken? What do I want? Where am I focusing? Each day, one moment at a time, I place my focus on what I have—focusing on hope and gratitude. I am still here, and I will keep reaching for what I know is there. I have no doubt. I am not broken, only severed from my norm. I have my husband, my family, my friends. I have my mind, my will, my ability to create my life, and my thoughts. I am directing the boat of my life.

Each one of us has the ability to make choices. Even when our choices may seem limited, we can dig deep and rev our engines. We can look at options and decide not to allow Fear to direct our lives. As we know, when Fear sets the direction of our boat, we end up hidden away, alone, sad, and disconnected. It is not the wake of our boat that sets our course; it is not the past of where we have been that is in charge. It is the driver, the observer who looks forward into the future and moves with possibility of life and adventure. As the driver, I am taking control and making decisions. While the motor powers the boat in the present, I am reminded it is not the wake that is in control. The past and the wake are not part of the directing factors. As I look at the present, I can appreciate where I am and what I have. I can look forward into the expanse in front of me and recognize options and horizons.

The doctors have said it is a miracle I am alive. I remember when I was young, I looked for the shape and design to life. So much of what has happened has felt like an accident. So maybe my path is my own and still unfilled, even if I can't see it yet.

The light slowly and gently seeps in fuzzy around the edges as my eyes work to focus on my tasks. My husband's eyes are gentle, but as I take him in, I see the concern. Tiredness seeps out from around his edges, rumpled clothing, bags, and laptops, fast food nearby—the sunlight streams in from the window.

Around me, the room gradually grows and clears.

I am still here.

CHAPTER FORTY-THREE

NEUROPLASTICITY

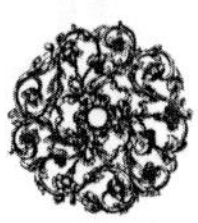

Our brains renew themselves throughout life to an extent previously not thought possible.

—Michael S. Gazzaniga

The more you ask, the more your mind can open. The more your thoughts grow to what you prefer, the more they can change the mind. We can develop the neurons in our brain, like plants spinning roots into the earth. Each thought is like a growing plant. It is a growing entity we can nurture. We can choose to water the brain's positive and preferred cognitive aspects improving the emotional elements. The mind allows the brain to change. We now know that the way we think changes the brain. It will change aspects of our brain and brain activities. If you believe you will not make it, then you will not make it. If you think you will make it, then the opportunity "to make it" opens up to you.

What we know is the brain is changing continuously. Twenty-five years ago, we thought that the brain did not change except to decrease. We thought the brain decreased as we aged. We now know this is not true. Whether we are ten years old or eighty years old, experiment after experiment has shown that our brains grow and evolve. Chemical changes go across neurons and throughout our brain structure. Long-term memory will allow these chemicals to move across the brain, altering its function from our behavior and thoughts. The more we use these parts of our brain, the more they become enhanced.

If you are a London taxi driver and you need to know the city, your brain will grow to allow this information to be available and to be accessible to you. If you are in flight or fight, your brain will grow to continue to protect you from the threat imagined or not. If you are in pain, your brain will grow to feel those pain neurons more, even as the pain may lessen.

The best driver of neuroplasticity is the use of "behavior" to rewire your brain. It is the constant change of behavior that allows the brain to grow. There is nothing more effective than practice to change the structure of the brain. Our actions, walking in the unknown, pushing ourselves to find the outcome rather than the pre-assumed outcome of the past, allow this growth to occur—this is where we grow. When we are no longer directed by what we "feel," but jump into finding out what can be, this is real growth. When we bypass our feelings and jump into our lives, we can finally find ourselves.

Life coach and author Mel Robbins uses the five-second rule. Counting ourselves down—*five, four, three, two, one*—and then stepping into life. Don't think about how it feels. Don't allow the hesitation to derail you. Walk into the situation and work to use your logic, not your feelings, to decide on the new behaviors. There is no size that fits all. There is only practice in our minds and with our bodies that allows change to occur.

This means walking into new, unfamiliar situations. Over and over again, allowing you to move into new behaviors and new brain structures. If you want to change what your brain is experiencing and the chemicals your brain is producing, this means you need to do the work and walk into new and different behaviors. Practice something new and different. Practice every day something that is scary because it is not familiar, or Fear will decide what the future brings. Find a physical, emotional, or mental risk that aligns with your values. Practice every day to see what will happen if you try this alignment. Become curious. Remember, everything you do and everything you experience is changing your brain. Decide to change it for the better rather than for a horrid known past.

Neuroplasticity is the brain's ability to create new pathways based on new experiences. It refers to changes in these pathways and synapses that result from changes in behavior and neural thought processes. New experiences can be thoughts or behaviors. The choice is yours. If you want options that will allow you to experience control, select these choices, and then notice how these choices give you options. If you are continually saying, "No, that will not work," you have shut yourself out of allowing options. If it hasn't worked in the past, try again.

Open yourself up to more information. Why and what can you do differently? What about it did not work? Do you have hard evidence to support your assumptions? Remember, feelings are *not hard evidence*. You can survive your emotions. Feelings have never killed anyone. You can feel like you're going to pass out, you're going to go crazy, you may even feel as though your heart is pounding. Again, these are feelings. They are uncomfortable, nothing more. And no one has died from being uncomfortable.

Dr. Joe Dispenza says, "If you can't overcome an old emotion, then you can't create anything new because that emotion is keeping you connected to the past." If you are determined and unburdened, you can release yourself and lead yourself with conviction. Using functional brain scans, we can see that talking about trauma and the past begins to release emotions, but you need to step into new thoughts and behaviors if you want to make changes.

If you continue down the path of feeding the monster of the past as your only option for the future, you will find you will lose interest in anything other than feeding this emotion. You will continue to provide for this emotion and feeling with past information as though it is future information. Inevitably, you will start to rationalize why the future is only a reflection of experiences you have had in the past. There are no other options to see and take in. The incidents that have happened to you will become so set in stone, Fear will stop you from experiencing anything new. You will rationalize why nothing can deviate from this, and therefore there is no growth. You visualize yourself and everyone locked into a repetitive response that allows for no free will. Nobody has the ability to react in any other way than what and how you have decided they are allowed to react.

Yet the more you are curious, the more questions you ask, and the more you work, the more your thoughts can grow and become ones you prefer—the more they can change the mind and your outcomes. We can grow the neurons in our brain like plants. The mind allows the brain to change and grow.

Stating we do not have an ability to learn and grown, that we are locked into a place of no free will, disregards all the learning we have encountered and used in our lives. Growth within our brain has allowed us to decide what we like and prefer and learn to change what we do not. It is an intrinsic property we have been gifted with: gifted with the free will to add and grow and change. Even the computers we build use information to learn, add into their systems, and change. If we did not know we had this ability, we would not have considered adding this into our technology.

When one becomes so overwhelmed with living in the automatic world of emotions—literally walking in a trance—we can reach for other tools that surpass the programming. Brainspotting and hypnotherapy are therapeutic techniques that allow the unconscious mind to release the emotions and form new and useful understandings of memory versus living in a fight-or-flight situation that no longer exists. "It is about lowering the emotion," says Dr. Dispenza. It is not about the event or the illness, but the emotions and feelings attached to that event or illness. As you recondition your mind, and realign the existing schemas and beliefs, you take back control and relearn how to be in the present moment. Then the body can begin to finally heal. The body no longer experiences the stress of the past, made-up situations, or a pretend "what if" future. In the present, it can relax and maintain calm. It is no longer feeding the monster of the past. It is no longer supporting and nurturing the unhealthy emotions that have kept one from moving into creating a new feeling, a new emotion, and health.

When we sit and ask ourselves, "Why am I feeling this? What is driving this feeling? What was I feeling before this trigger or situation? Was I feeling better? Which would I prefer? What emotion would I choose to walk into?"—and most importantly, "Is this what I want to be feeling?"—these types of self-exploration questions can open you to an enhanced or preferred emotion. Look at how your sentiment changes when you are curious rather than holding the old feeling. What happened when you allowed the feeling to change to curiosity? Now you are able to ask yourself, is there a response to the new information that you want to increase? Does it feel better? Has the information provided a different direction or feeling?

We can choose to feed the good wolf or the bad, the response or the reaction. Which one do you want to grow? Which neural network are you enhancing? Are you feeding your reaction and your feelings, or are you feeding your response to information and your understanding? Which part of your brain are you growing, and what is your choice? If it is to be less anxious, you can work to rewire the brain. You can change the chemicals and the functioning of the brain. Listen to Anxiety, follow its lead, remember it is telling you that something is off.

Remember, the sympathetic nervous system can be turned on to send messages that are not accurate. When this happens, you are watering the wrong plant. If you continue to avoid, react to old patterns, or listen only to your feelings, you will continue to feed and water the plant of the past. In other words, the old neural network that no longer works for you will grow strong and secure. The more you ask, the more you work. The more you step into the unknown, your thoughts can grow toward what you prefer and thus the more you can change the neural network of your mind.

Are you growing new parts of your brain? Or will you interpret others to react as you have decided they will and only will? If this decision is made, it is at this point that the mind is no longer the mind, but instead becomes the body. The body that is directing you with feelings. Stop and ask yourself how meaningful is this reaction to you? Emotion is speaking to your cells, and your genes are now responding to this information. Notice whether illness befalls. Physical or mental, they are interconnected in so many ways, for we cannot disconnect the mind from the body. Know you can still reach for truth, hope, and self-belief.

If you want to change what your brain is experiencing, or the chemicals your brain is producing, you need to do the work and to walk into new and different thoughts and behaviors. Practice, practice, practice something new and different. Practice every day something that is unfamiliar yet aligned with your values. Practice every day to see what will happen if you try. Become curious. Everything you do and everything you think is changing your brain.

Decide what wolf you are going to feed. What reality are you going to experience? What neural pathway are you going to grow? How are you choosing to be in this world? What will you practice? As Prem Rawat, a global ambassador who advanced peace and dignity, says:

> *"Do you practice happiness? Do you practice peace, or do you practice worry? Because if you practice worry you will get very good at it. You will get so good at it you will worry about everything. Even when there's nothing for a layman to worry over, for you will become an expert in worry. You will even worry about that which is not yours."*

For more information on practicing a new story rather than a familiar old one, go to www.HelloAnxiety.net.

CHAPTER FORTY-FOUR

LOVE STORY

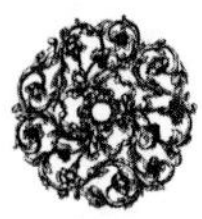

Nothing celebrates life, celebrates wisdom, celebrates truth, like the heart. Nothing!

—Prem Rawat

My husband loves to tell the story of how he wooed me. As his story goes, he fell in love with me long before I fell in love with him. Wide-eyed and tentative, he watched me from afar. Giddy when we could spend time together at college, he kept up hope that he would one day be with me, but he never let me know. So I, of course, thought of him only as this cute guy who wanted just to be friends. Dancing around our feelings for each other as we waltzed in and out of places, events, and encounters, seven years later we found ourselves walking down the aisle surrounded by friends and family.

My friends knew it was serious when I drove from Nags Head, North Carolina, to Athens, Georgia, and back again in three days just to have him meet my "Beach Crowd." A long journey filled with anticipation as the car bumped along the road, music streaming out the windows. We sang and laughed toward our destination, open and free as only youth can capture. Thankfully, once we arrived, he passed the friend test. He liked them, and they liked him. The important people in my life connected and appreciated each other. We could relax into acceptance, enjoying ourselves. My friends are very much family to me, and having love, friends, and laughter all together is one of my needs. One that I prefer.

Remember, your needs are required. They are a necessity. You must have them to exist. When I had what we call the "event"—clot and embolism—my husband and family suddenly experienced a lack of "water." Remember, without water, our existence is limited. Water is representative of our needs and control. When we are in charge of our own needs and do not place that control externally, those needs can be met. One's circle of control includes thoughts, efforts, behaviors, and feelings.

So, for my husband, the everyday life, the comings and goings, the humdrum of ordinary thoughts, efforts, and behaviors flew out the window as our proverbial pipes broke.

My husband had to take the brunt of my trauma. Each image burnt into his brain connected to pain and helplessness. He witnessed both cardiac arrests. He saw me stop breathing, and he witnessed the ferocious seizures. On the sidelines, as the paramedics worked to keep me alive, he saw the hospital staff and me trying to fight—the machines, the noise, the commotion, the instant of change and helplessness.

He was there when they intubated me, when they were fighting to regain my life, when they were pushing chemicals into my body to break apart the massive embolism that had filled both chambers of my lungs and then my heart. He witnessed me bleeding out as the blood poured out from every opening, soaking through the bed and sheets. And he was there when they froze my body, placing me in a coma.

When they lowered my core temperature in an attempt to save brain function, he was there as the staff told him I might not ever wake up. If I did, I might not know who he was. I may not be able to care for myself. I may have to re-learn how to walk, talk, eat, and bathe. I may not ever leave the bed. Everything was unknown. It was a breeding ground for Fear, Anxiety, worry, loss, grief—no control. Only hope attempted to hang on by the thread of love.

When the floor falls out from under us, we suddenly realize the intensity of our needs. How much we rely on those needs being met and accessible, how each need has been an essential part of our day, our being, our existence. Without them, we are off. We want to have our moments and connection once again in our lives.

Thankfully, two days after the emergency room visit, a head nurse took my husband aside and gave him the ins and outs of what to expect. He had been struggling to maintain a sense of balance. Finally, having information and beginning to see that there was still a possibility for me to come around, he was better able to regain focus and hang on. There are always ways and things to explore, learn, and hope for.

The fear of losing our family, our connection, and our love loomed heavily over him. Still, the information he received sitting in the sterile room, ferreted away from the hospital staff's hustle and bustle, helped him open up possibilities, and these choices began to push down the Fear.

Standing in line, each COVID question correctly answered brought him closer and closer to the halls and rooms spanning in front of him. He went through the protocols, the demands for safety, and early morning risings to be with me and sit by my side once they began to warm me up degree by degree. The sun would have set and the darkness settled down over the cars when they would tell him to go home. Exhausted, emotionally drained, he would update our friends and loved ones till the wee hours, then turn around to arrive and start all over again the next morning.

He brought the staff donuts, and bagels, and sandwich trays. Sticky and gooey, freshly made, the smell would call the nursing staff to his arrival. He made sure they knew who I was and that the care they gave was appreciated. He was my knight, my angel, my constant. Our family surrounded him, keeping him propped up and covering his wearied body when he finally relinquished himself to exhaustion. Our friends sat by his side as he wept and struggled through the unknown of what lay ahead. And yet he worked to keep our proverbial water flowing at the house and in the hospital.

Finally, they stopped the sedation. They began to warm up my body and my brain.

"Can you move a toe?" . . . I did.

"Can you move your finger?" . . . I did

They removed the intubation tubes and placed me on oxygen . . . I spoke two words.

I was there, and I was fighting in my own way. My brain and body were slowly coming back online as though from a massive panic attack. My body knew I could not take another explosive event, so it worked slowly and steadily. My brain also knew I did not need to focus on the past, where I had been, but focus on where I was going.

My memory was hazy, my mind trying to reconnect. My body was wanting to move yet still unable. The weight of me was intense. But I knew I was here. I was loved. I was supported, yet apparently, there was still something God or the Universe had in mind for me to do.

I was coming back slowly. It was a miracle.

CHAPTER FORTY-FIVE

CHANGE IS POSSIBLE

Speak with your words and your message can be distorted . . . Speak with your actions and leave no doubt.

—Dr. Steve Maraboli

When we act differently, walk into a situation rather than run from it, think about logic and curiosity, we will water a new neural pathway. We calm the sympathetic nervous system. We activate healing and digestion. We begin to program our brains to respond differently and send different chemicals to grow and change. We change the makeup and chemical output of our brains.

We have witnessed this over and over again. Scientists watch the brain rewire. It does not matter if you are young or old. The brain has the capacity to learn and grow. It has the ability to change. Changing patterns and behaviors is not easy, but it is possible. It may not be easy for a child to learn multiplication tables, but it is possible. It may not be easy to walk forward when you feel anxious and learn to become curious opening yourself up to something else, but it is possible. It takes practice and a willingness and desire to stop your automatic pattern when you hear Anxiety. Notice when your friend Anxiety is talking to you. Recognize when they want to get your attention. Stop, listen to what Fear is saying, and choose to say something new. Do something different. Ground yourself and move forward with curiosity.

So, what is grounding and how do you do it? Here is a simple exercise to put you in the moment and allow your nervous system to reestablish safety:

Grounding Exercise:

Count down starting at five and notice:

Five things you can see.
Four things you can feel.
Three things you can hear.
Two things you can smell.
One thing you can taste.

Once you are in the present, step forward. Remember how being present helps you to run from the thought, not the situation. Decide to move forward toward the opposite of what you typically do. If you avoid or run away from others, go toward them, and be curious about them. Decide how you feel about them once you have precise information about who they are now, after you have spent time with them, not before. Do not judge.

Suppose you get overwhelmed and start to raise your voice and yell. Notice what about these reactions pushes people away. If you want them to hear you and understand you, then stop, ground yourself with *five-four-three-two-one,* then say how you feel and ask for what you want rather than yelling and anger. If you want connection and understanding, then do not yell and push them away with intense emotions.

If you reach for alcohol because the stress is too much, reach out and hold someone close. Maybe tell someone you're afraid to fail, or maybe tell someone you need his or her help. Ask to be loved even if you screw up. Remember, you are not your feelings.

You can make a mistake—that doesn't make you a mistake. You can fail at something, and it doesn't make you a failure. Humans are fallible not perfect. You can respond differently.

If you shut down and find you cannot respond or share your feelings, notice how this is protecting you and stopping you from fulfilling your needs. It is not allowing your needs to be heard, seen, and acknowledged. I love the five-second rule by Mel Robbins. She was in a place where she felt lost, failing, scared, and depressed, with no motivation to move forward. She had hit bottom. Suddenly, it came to her to start counting down like a rocket being shot into space, "five-four-three-two-one," and take a step toward what she couldn't do: pick up the phone, look for a job, ask for help, get up and get dressed, open up rather than shut down. Mel counted and then started moving, breaking the feeling habits by shifting her behavior five seconds at a time.

There is so much research on this five-second method, and many people have used the rocket analogy to begin the movement of their new lives. They are walking away from having their feelings dictate their every mood and behavior. They have stopped indecision from unraveling their sense of inner knowing. They dislodged the seed of doubt from taking root in their brain to grow Fear. They, too, have started walking into their desires and needs, allowing something new to dictate their actions five seconds at a time while changing their brains and behaviors by embracing something other than Fear.

You, too, can begin to grow something new in your life. Change your brain and allow yourself to find happiness.

Five seconds at a time.

For more grounding techniques, check out www.HelloAnxiety.net.

CHAPTER FOURTY-SIX

REHABILITATION

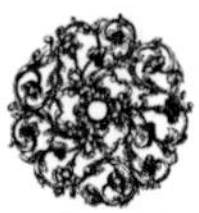

A dream you dream alone is only a dream. A dream you dream together is reality.

—John Lennon

He was quiet in his deliberate caring voice, speaking of our time and the beauty we had held. The time felt brief and yet expansive for him, encompassing more than he or I alone. The energy between us, greater than the sum of ourselves. I saw my husband as he gazed out over the expanse.

"She slipped away in October. And she doesn't even know that she is gone."

Moving to rehabilitation was so fulfilling. I was finally able to reach, grow, and be challenged. The hospital doctors were cautious, and I was pushing. As I look back, I now understand their reasons for concern and caution. But in the moment, I let it wash away. *I got this! Let me get on and get going!*

Moving me from one hospital to another allowed me to feel the air, the freshness outside, and the sun. *Oh so glorious.* My family could not visit because of the COVID pandemic, but they were given a heads-up about my departure time. The pavement beneath their feet and with the trees' shade on their backs, they waited outside near the ambulance, hoping to see me and grab a hug.

Wheels flowing down the halls, then onto the sidewalk, my gurney approached the doors. And then there they were, my family, all smiles mingled with concern. Quietly stepping away, the ambulance crew gave us a few moments to exchange love and well wishes, an opportunity for my children and parents to size up my state of being and get a personal assessment of my progress. We shared our joy and appreciation of this precious moment for each other before the next leg in the journey. Though brief, this moment was healing and reassuring for me and my family.

Bumpy roads meant we meandered down the highway and onto small streets, attempting to escape traffic and roadblocks. The driver did a great job as the paramedic in the ambulance, sat with me in the back. I asked him how he came to be caring for others and me. Young and full of direction, it was interesting to hear how he once felt he was lost and struggling. His path had been muddled as he pursued something more out of societal obligation rather than the comfort of self-direction. He had suddenly experienced a challenge, which helped him to redirect. It created fulfillment, synchronistic in nature. It moved him toward this direction. He then grabbed on and moved forward. Now he was completing paramedic training, fireman training, and ambulance service. A brotherhood of support surrounded him, helped him, and shared information with him, keeping him engaged. This direction allowed him to meet new people out in the world versus in an office. He enjoyed camping and hiking, and doing anything in the great outdoors, and he found he could use these skills to help others.

As I listened, I thought of others in my life that may appreciate his insight and may want to hear his story. He was thrilled, as he viewed it as a gift to give and share his information with others, mentoring them if they allowed. He loved to help other people find if this path may also speak to them. I noticed the synchronistic nature of our moment and grabbed it as I could. The meaning was not lost on me: the people we encounter and the appreciation of these moments. The importance hopefully not lost on those who could benefit from his courageous ability to grab onto his truth and his pathway.

The clock read 3:33 when I arrived. Repetitive numbers seem to follow me. I feel as though God and my angels are speaking and sending me messages that they are with me, watching over me. The number 333 is a message of encouragement that all things are possible through persistence and a positive mindset. It is a message of comfort, letting me know that I have inner strength and to keep going my way. I am reminded that I can change my world, whether facing health issues, hopelessness, or setbacks, by changing the way I think and how I view this moment and the future. I embraced the numbers and said a private prayer of thanks, gleefully pointing out the numbers to my husband as they wheeled me away from the strength of his presence into the elevator.

Loud and insistent, the helicopter landed on the roof of the building across from my window. Dirty and dusty, I could still make out the sign of the Children's Hospital glowing through the breaking dawn. Early light began to grow as the staff opened the door to draw blood once again, take my vitals, and raise my bed. It was five a.m., and my day was beginning. My schedule was filled: occupational therapy for one hour, physical therapy for one hour, a neurocognitive exam for two hours, lunch, doctor visit, recreation therapy for one hour, and finally one more hour of physical therapy before I could be wheeled back into my bed for dinner.

Exhausted and drained, I would struggle to operate the remote control and open my plastic forks and knives. Each day, five a.m. would roll around, and I would once again go through the routine. Finally, on Sunday, I was allowed a day off. It was so needed and refreshing for my body and mind. The staff recognized my potassium was very low, which was causing my inability to move and operate my hands, legs, and fingers. Who knew that potassium is the wonder mineral that allows these brain connections to occur? Fortunately, the medical staff did. Eight hours of transfusion suddenly found me picking up my fork, holding the remote, pushing buttons on my phone. A whole old world opened back up for me.

Next came the drop in blood sugar. Shaking with exhaustion, the staff checked my numbers, and sure enough, my levels were very low. My energy returned after adding sugar and peanut butter into my body, as I experienced my focus increase.

The hospital staff worked to allow my body to find and access the nutrients needed to reestablish brain connections as I worked to find my voice and dexterity. Each day, I pushed a little more as they watched like a hawk over my heart, blood pressure, and oxygen levels. We had a few scares, but they caught each one. The highlight was when they took a video for my family on my phone. Walking on my own for ten feet, I then climbed eight steps up and down to my delight and the staff's. Sharing the video with my family filled me with joy as they exclaimed with unbelief at my progress.

I worked hard for three weeks and, each evening, listened to meditations of healing and growth. My dreams were filled with visions of the future—a future of laughter, running, and open spaces. I knew to envision this future as my "now." And use my Anxiety and my brain to reorganize and reconnect the wiring within.

Once I was home, I woke up rattled by the dream of my husband gazing out over life, my loss, and death. Hearing my husband's voice still in my head, it permeated the sheets as I substantiated my existence and questioned my reality. I could still feel the anguish as I swirled into this existence away from my dream. My husband's hand crept close, grabbing mine, grounding me in the bed and in the world. Still asleep, he felt my confusion and need as his hand and warmth held me here in our mutual dream of reality.

I did not slip away in October. I am still here.

EPILOGUE

RESOLVE

Sometimes you can't see what you're learning until you come out the other side.

—Gal Gadot, *Wonder Woman 1984*

Most people do not know I am still struggling. My friends call me a "wonder woman," and my doctors have picked up on the nickname. I find it amusing and endearing. My superpower is my friend Anxiety. A strange but oh-so-useful power, it helps keep me in check and keeps me reaching for new adventures. I can only hope that others learn to harness their own ability within and to experience what my old friend Anxiety has allowed me to understand. It is so misunderstood, yet so faithful. Anxiety has guided me, and it is there also trying to guide you.

I still have trouble moving, writing, and, at times, finding my words, but I am not alone. I miss not being able to sing, having lost the resonance and tone of my voice. At times, it fills me with sadness, these losses I have yet to reestablish—yet I have a wonderful sense of magic and eight miracles to remind me of how I am still here, how I am loved. And along the way, I have been reminded of how I often I have felt alone and how wrong I have been. My feelings had me stray from the truth. My truth is I have felt the love of family, of friends, of clients, and strangers. I have experienced the love of hospital staff, grocery clerks, and ambulance workers. I have reconnected in so many ways with the love Anxiety is pointing all of us toward. Like a guiding light toward self and soul, Anxiety has opened me up to vulnerability and growth.

I set off in writing this book to gather and place together skills for others to begin to understand how their Anxiety is a gift, an experience, and a friend dedicated to reminding us we are here together and cared for deeply. Anxiety will always be available for us to talk with. Anxiety is not a quiet guide, but it is constant and present to alert us when we have stepped off our path. Our path to find self-love and inclusion. Helping us to learn what control truly is. Learning we are loved and how utilizing this superpower can change our world.

This book has been more than skills and understanding. It has been an opportunity for me to reestablish my own sense of knowing. What is real, what are the rules of this world, what is consciousness? I feel I have a knowing that is mine. Others may not understand, may judge, it may fill some with fear. But my knowing is solid. I see and understand it, and it is not necessary for me to shout out to the world how I have made sense of the miracles I have encountered, but to hold a space for others to find their own sense of knowing—their own truth, their own worth—and experience their own miracle as I walk with them on their path.

I have lived eight miracles and I hope to heck the next one comes in forty years when I'm ready for my next adventure. I look forward to encountering this time as an opportunity to watch my children and clients grow. Looking back, I know I resolved my panic attacks, my cancer, my embolism, my cardiac arrest, firmly stepped into faith rather than doubt, and embraced my understanding of internal, physical, and mental control versus external control. I am able to hold a space for others to understand their own journey and be with them as they embrace their path without fear. Watching them embrace their possibilities and superpower, breaking the habits that have held them hostage, renews my faith each day.

Let's step out together, into a world with your superpower Anxiety by your side.

Step into your own miracles.

You are not alone.

BIBLIOGRAPHY

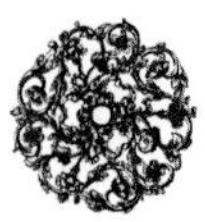

"7 Bible Verses about Faith Moving Mountains." Knowing Jesus. Accessed on November 7, 2022. https://bible.knowing-jesus.com/topics/Faith-Moving-Mountains.

Ackerman, C. "What is Neuroplasticity? A Psychologist Explains [+14 Exercises]." PositivePsychology.com. July 25, 2018). https://positivepsychology.com/neuroplasticity/.

Anderson, Greg. "Greg Anderson Quotes." BrainyQuote. Accessed November 28, 2021. www.brainyquote.com/quotes/greg_anderson_642636.

Aristotle. Teachings. Stagira: 340 BC.

"Blood clot in lung: Should you worry?" MyHeart. January 22, 2016. https://myheart.net/articles/blood-clot-in-lung-should-you-worry/.

Brown, B. "Daring Greatly: How the Courage to Be Vulnerable Transforms the Way We Live, Love, Parent, and Lead." Gotham Books, 2012.

Brown, S. "Consequences of Play Deprivation." Scholarpedia 9, no. 5, (2014): 30449. https://doi.org/10.4249/scholarpedia.30449

Chopra, Deepak. Spiritual Solutions : Answers to Life's Greatest Challenges. New York: Harmony Books, 2012.

Chung, Kristin. "Selective Attention Test 2.0." YouTube. 31 Oct. 2012, www.youtube.com/watch?v=z9aUseqgCiY. Accessed 15 Dec. 2020.

CRS Report. "Unemployment Rates during the COVID-19 Pandemic: In Brief." Congressional Research Service. Updated on

March 12, 2021. https://crsreports.congress.gov/product/pdf/R/R46554/9.

Dispenza, J., & Amen, D. G. Breaking the Habit of Being Yourself: How to Lose Your Mind and Create a New One. Hay House, 2015.

Dr, G. E. Life Script Restructuring: The Neuroplastic Psychology for Rewiring Your Brain and Changing Your Life. Aphalon Firth, 2014.

Ahmed, Mustafa. "Pulmonary Embolism - The Killer Clot in the Lungs." MyHeart. January 20, 2016. https://myheart.net/articles/pulmonary-embolism-the-killer-clot-in-the-lungs/.

Dyer, Wayne. "Motivational Quotes - Dr. Wayne Dyer." YouTube. www.youtube.com/watch?v=QaAz4novu58.

Epel, E. S., Blackburn, E. H., Lin, J., Dhabhar, F. S., Adler, N. E., Morrow, J. D., & Cawthon, R. M. "Accelerated telomere shortening in response to life stress." Proceedings of the National Academy of Sciences 101, no. 49, (2004): 17312–17315. https://doi.org/10.1073/pnas.0407162101.

Shinn, Florence Scovel. The Game of Life and How to Play It. Mockingbird Press, 2021.

"folklore - What is the folkloristic origin of cats having 9 lives?" Mythology & Folklore Stack Exchange. Retrieved June 28, 2021. https://mythology.stackexchange.com/questions/1843/what-is-the-folkloristic-origin-of-cats-having-9-lives.

foresthealer. "Forest Bathing – What, How, Where? A beginner's guide." Healing Forest, January 27, 2020. https://healingforest.org/2020/01/27/forest-bathing-guide/.

Gazzaniga, M. S. Who's In charge? Free Will and the Science of the Brain. London Robinson, 2016.

Gorkonel, D. "250+ [BEST] Encouraging Good Night Quotes & Wishes." Awesoroo. 2019. https://awesoroo.com/100-best-encouraging-good-night-quotes-this-year#inspirational.

Hanai, A., Ishiguro, H., Sozu, T., Tsuda, M., Yano, I., Nakagawa, T., Imai, S., Hamabe, Y., Toi, M., Arai, H., & Tsuboyama, T. "Effects of Cryotherapy on Objective and Subjective

Symptoms of Paclitaxel-Induced Neuropathy: Prospective Self-Controlled Trial." JNCI: Journal of the National Cancer Institute 110, no. 2, (2017): 141–148. https://doi.org/10.1093/jnci/djx178.

Hay, L. L. You Can Heal Your Life. 2003.

"Jon Kabat-Zinn - 'the Healing Power of Mindfulness.'" YouTube. www.youtube.com/watch?v=_If4a-gHg_I. Accessed October 30, 2021.

Katie, B. "The Work Of Byron Katie."

Lightning Process, Neuroplasticity and anxiety. Ian Cleary. Accessed October 29, 2022. http://iancleary.com/category/neuroplasticity-anxiety-depression/.

"Love yourself like your life depends on it; because it DOES | Anita Moorjani." YouTube. Accessed October 30, 2022. https://www.youtube.com/watch?v=iokctou6NhI

Leadem, Rose. "10 Powerful Quotes From Hollywood Star, Producer, Philanthropist and Entrepreneur Reese Witherspoon." Entrepreneur. March 22, 2018. https://www.entrepreneur.com/leadership/10-powerful-quotes-from-hollywood-star-producer/310666.

Leaf, C. Switch on Your Brain Workbook: The Key to Peak Happiness, Thinking, and Health. Baker Books, 2017.

Milne, A. A., & Shepard, E. H. The Complete Tales & Poems of Winnie-the-Pooh. Dutton Children's Books, 2001.

Mitchell, S. "Theory of Natural Connection [Review of Theory of Natural Connection]." The Search for Why - Pop-Up Magazine 43, (2020). https://www.popupmagazine.com/yearinsearch.pdf.

Bowen, Tom. "Five Things I Wish I Knew Earlier in My Journey with Chronic Pain." STAT. August 12, 2019. https://www.statnews.com/2019/08/12/chronic-pain-journey-five-things-understand/.

News-Democrat (TNS), R. S. B. "Why do we say cats have nine lives?" Dispatch Argus. Accessed July 1, 2021. https://qconline.com/lifestyles/pets/why-do-we-say-cats-have-nine-lives/article_085e1cff-8764-55f9-a1de-fbff7442e194.html#:~:text=ANSWER%3A%20Historians%20say%20the%20Egyptians.

"Pain: What it is and how to treat it." August 28, 2020. www.medicalnewstoday.com.

Richo, D. When Love Meets Fear: Becoming Defenseless and Resourceful. Satprakashan Sanchar Kendra, 2001.

Robbins, M. Summary: The 5 Second Rule. Monee, Il: Epicread, 2019.

Schumaker, Lisa. "Global Coronavirus Deaths Exceed 700,000, One Person Dies Every 15 Seconds on Average." Reuters. August 5, 2020. https://www.reuters.com/article/health-coronavirus-casualties/global-coronavirus-deaths-exceed-700000-one-person-dies-every-15-seconds-on-average-idUKL1N2F602X.

Siegel, Daniel J. Mindsight: The New Science of Personal Transformation. Carlton North, Vic.: Scribe Publications, 2009.

Socrates. (430 BC). Musings. Athens: 430 BC.

Strayed, C. Tiny Beautiful Things: Advice On Love and Life From Dear Sugar. Vintage Books, 2012.

Vadoa, E. A., Hall, C. R., & Moritz, S. E. "The relationship between competitive anxiety and imagery use." Journal of Applied Sport Psychology 9, no. 2, (1997): 241–253. https://doi.org/10.1080/10413209708406485.

"what do you practice (Pearls of wisdom by great guide Prem Rawat-we are forever grateful to him." YouTube. Accessed July 1, 2021. https://www.youtube.com/watch?v=53cqxEOuHNI&list=PLnOPU0ztZ7TWr82nFamx3_mnfUTnVXFH8&index=4&t=2s.

Yano, J. M., Yu, K., Donaldson, G. P., Shastri, G. G., Ann, P., Ma, L., Nagler, C. R., Ismagilov, R. F., Mazmanian, S. K., & Hsiao, E. Y. "Indigenous bacteria from the gut microbiota regulate host serotonin biosynthesis. "Cell 161, no. 2, (2015): 264–276. https://doi.org/10.1016/j.cell.2015.02.047.

Zettle, R. D. ACT for Depression: A Clinician's Guide to Using Acceptance & Commitment Therapy In Treating Depression. New Harbinger Publications, 2007.

About the Author

Natalie Kohlhaas is an anxiety specialist, clinical therapist, counselor, and seminar leader. She is widely known for her work with anxiety disorders and therapeutic techniques for those clients with whom talk therapy "has failed." She has attended and graduated with degrees in psychology from Oxford College of Emory University, the University of Georgia, and Georgia School of Professional Psychology. Her training with David Grand for brainspotting and the Wellness Institute in clinical hypnotherapy has helped to shift the emotional residue of many clients and therapists. She has held multiple board positions and engaged in speaking opportunities. Currently, she sits on the Licensed Professional Counselor Board for Georgia addressing supervision issues. Natalie has not only worked to train individuals, therapists, and families, but she has also worked with hospitals, the Department of Family and Children Services, and the National Institute of Mental Health to formulate studies and procedures for of those who are in need.

With a background deeply rooted in tradition, she has integrated her wide-ranging experience into a program of psychological development and integrative mental health. Her working evidence-based model is founded not only on brain-based information but incorporates nutritional and healthy lifestyle elements where the mind, body, and spirit are addressed and released into their ability to heal, finding their place to exist within and without.

Natalie has been in practice for over twenty-four years and has had a multitude of working experiences, all of which have helped to form the individual she is today.

As of the printing of this book, her current licensure and certifications include:

- National Board-Certified Counselor
- Certified Clinical Behavioral-Hypnotherapist
- Licensed Professional Counselor (Georgia)
- Certified Professional Counselor Supervisor
- National Board-Certified Fellow in Clinical Hypnotherapy
- Certified Specialist in Hypnosis and PTSD
- Certified Instructor of Hypnosis
- Chi Sigma Iota Member